FAMOUS REGIMENTS

Queen Alexandra's Royal Army Nursing Corps

FAMOUS REGIMENTS

Edited by
Lt-General Sir Brian Horrocks

Queen Alexandra's Royal Army Nursing Corps

by
Juliet Piggott

Leo Cooper Ltd, London

First published in Great Britain 1975
by Leo Cooper Ltd,
196 Shaftesbury Avenue,
London WC2H 8JL

Copyright © 1975 by Juliet Piggott

Introduction Copyright © 1975
by Lt-General Sir Brian Horrocks

ISBN 0 85052 193 9

Printed in Great Britain by
Clarke, Doble & Brendon Ltd,
Plymouth

In memory of my mother

Contents

Illustrations

Foreword

There were several delights in the writing of this book, but there were two main difficulties. The first was that neither the QAIMNS nor the QARANC has an Official History. The second was that, in common with other corps in the British Army, QAs have served, and are serving still, wherever the British Army is stationed. They have never all been in a specific place at a specific time: they have been widely dispersed at all times.

In order to give their story any form I relied on a variety of works. The most helpful, apart from those mentioned in the text, were *The Royal Army Medical Corps* by Redmond McLaughlin, *Not Least In The Crusade* by Peter Lovegrove, *Aldershot Review* by John Walters, *Florence Nightingale* by Cecil Woodham-Smith and *Catharine Grace Loch: A Memoir*.

I was greatly helped by the access I was given to the Minutes of the Nursing Board and other papers, diaries and correspondence by AMD4, Ministry of Defence, the QARANC Museum in Aldershot and the Royal Army Medical College Library at Millbank. The ready assistance that Mrs E. Fifield at AMD4, Mrs J. Churchill in Aldershot and Mr M. M. Davies at Millbank gave me were among the pleasures I encountered during the course of my researches.

I am grateful too for the willing help given me by the Commonwealth War Graves Commission and the Directorate of History, Canadian Forces Headquarters, Ottawa.

Lt-Gen Sir Neil Cantlie and Major-Gen A. MacLennan both gave me assistance and advice which were invaluable.

Mr Ted Le Blanc Smith kindly gave me permission to quote from his late sister's last letter home. I am glad that our correspondence enabled him to learn how part of that letter came to appear in a previous publication.

Yet another delight was the large response from the United Kingdom and the Commonwealth to my letter asking for reminiscences. The list of my correpondents is too long to give in full: I have thanked each one individually. I am particularly grateful to Sister Mary Jordan, OP, Dame Barbara Cozens, Mrs W. M. Stewart, Mrs Irene Duncan, Miss Mary Wilson, Miss Kay Thomson, Miss K. G. Christie, Miss Rose Hinchey and Mr Charles Collins. They, over a period of many months, patiently and encouragingly answered my questions.

It was Brig Barbara Gordon who first thought of this book when she was Matron-in-Chief. She opened many doors to facilitate my research and my gratitude to her for doing this is genuine indeed.

Her successor, Brig Helen Cattanach, not only kept the doors ajar but unhesitatingly pushed them wider and opened others as the scope of my research widened. She, with Col Kay Grimshaw, the Commandant of the Training Centre at the Royal Pavilion, enabled me to stay and work in Aldershot on several occasions. For all this help, hospitality and transport I am much indebted. Indeed, without it, I could not have written the book.

Lastly I would thank the many QAs, whether retired or still serving, who have been so unstinting in their readiness to share with me their knowledge. Only a small selection of them will find their names in the text, but I like to believe that all of them were not only aware of my eagerness to catch and put on paper the spirit of the Corps, but actually enabled me to do it. If I have not got it right, the fault is mine, not theirs.

J.E.J.P.
Cranleigh,
Surrey.
August, 1974

Introduction

by Lt-General Sir Brian Horrocks

I am particularly glad to write an Introduction to this excellent account of the development of our Military Nursing Service, because the father of Juliet Piggott (Col F. S. G. Piggott, subsequently Major-General) was the first Senior Officer under whom I served in the War Office after leaving the Staff College. He proved to be a kindly, tolerant Commander, with a first-class brain. I can remember to this day the pained look which came into his eyes when I confessed, rather nervously, to having offered accelerated promotion by mistake to an officer who was dead.

Juliet Piggott has obviously inherited his numerous talents, and I would like to start by congratulating her on the vast amount of research which she must have undertaken in order to produce such a coherent, fascinating story of the development of our Military Nursing Service, known to my generation as the Queen Alexandra's Imperial Military Nursing Service. She describes with meticulous attention to detail the steady development of the military nursing services, and what makes her book so fascinating is her description of the different Matrons-in-Chief who emerge as the human milestones on the road towards the magnificent Corps which exists today: each contributed something to the formation of the best Army Medical Service in the world today.

It would be pointless for me to repeat what she has done so well. I will only say that I grew up with many of these famous names, as my father was in the RAMC. He was, in fact, the first Director of Hygiene, invented the Horrocks Box, and worked with Bruce in the discovery of the cause of Malta Fever. After retirement, he edited the RAMC Journal, and underwent two serious operations at Millbank Military Hospital where he was, of course, nursed by the QAs, for whom he developed a great admiration. It was here that I first came in contact with military nurses in their attractive grey uniforms, red capes and white caps, although it was not until the Second World War that I came into close contact with our own QAs in the Middle East.

After the Germans had been defeated in North Africa in 1943 I moved back with 10 Corps, which I was then commanding, in reserve to the Tripoli area. It was a very pleasant change, after many months of almost continuous active service. The whole Corps relaxed, re-fitted, re-organized and bathed, but by now Tripoli had become a main medical area, and some twelve base hospitals had been erected in the vicinity. Hospitals meant nurses, British and Dominion girls, whom many of the Corps had not even seen for a very long period indeed. Every evening, outside their camp, were parked rows and rows of jeeps, waiting to drive the nurses to parties in the different Officers' Messes. This was all very well, but it did not seem to me that the troops were getting their fair share. So I invited all the Matrons to lunch. This I regard as almost my bravest act of the war. I have always found one Matron frightening enough, but here I was, alone with *twelve*. However, they all responded nobly to my request that they should try and induce their nurses to attend twice-weekly dances for ORs only. These proved enormously successful, and it meant a great deal to the men who had not spoken to a British girl for a long time to be able to dance with one again. This is the other side of the picture: there is no doubt that particularly in isolated places, the presence of a few nurses was very good for morale.

A few weeks later I was to experience the professional side of nursing myself, as I was wounded in North Africa by a bullet from an enemy aircraft, which entered the top of my chest, and having passed through a number of organs inside me, eventually emerged at the bottom of my spine. I was rushed into an American Field Hospital on the outskirts of Bizerta, where I was operated on by an American surgeon, Col Carter from Dallas.

I occupied the corner of a General Ward, with a constantly changing population of troops from every country taking part in the war – friend and foe. The toughest of all were unquestionably the French Goumier, from the North African mountains, on whom pain and discomfort seemed to have no effect whatever.

Afer a few weeks I was flown back to the UK in an American bomber, as I had reached the stage where the facilities of a General Hospital were required. I found out afterwards that this had been specially arranged for me by Gen Bedell-Smith, Eisenhower's Chief-of-Staff. We landed at Farnborough, near Aldershot, and I was whisked into Cambridge Military Hospital. I now, for the first time, experienced the real efficiency of a top Harley Street Surgeon, Edward Muir, supported by first-class nursing. I was in that hospital, off and on, for fourteen months, and I have no doubt at all that my life was saved by Muir, and the selfless devotion of the British nurses, notably Miss Wilkinson and Miss Piercy.

Towards the end of my long period in the Cambridge I became a sort of tame parrot. Everyone knew me, and all sorts of people used to drop in for a chat. This had its amusing side. Many of the nurses had been invited to a New Year's Eve Dance in a nearby Officers' Mess, but had run into difficulties because it was decreed that everyone must be back in their quarters by 11 pm.

Eventually, a deputation of nurses came to see me. Their plan was simplicity itself. As all the doors would be closed to them after 11 pm, those wishing to return to the hospital in the early hours of the morning would get in through my window, which was conveniently placed on the ground-floor. No one in authority, they thought, would have any suspicion that the General's room was being used for this illicit purpose. I, of course, agreed, and all went well. Nurse after nurse returned successfully from the dance. Then came disaster – the Head Night-Sister spotted one of them emerging from the door of my room, and immediately gave chase. The nurse, being younger, gained a short lead, slipped into her room and jumped into bed. Sure enough, the door opened and in came the Sister. The nurse, apparently, put up a magnificent performance of a girl awaking from a deep sleep, but to no avail. The Sister merely said tartly, 'Do you usually go to bed with your hat on?' The poor nurse was on the mat next morning.

When I returned to the Battle in August 1944, and took over

command of XXX Corps in the Normandy Beachhead, the medical services of the British Expeditionary Force had reached perfection. The same Casualty Clearing Station always worked with my Corps, and as the key to the successful evacuation of casualties was speed, our CCS was always located within the shortest possible distance of the front line, well within range of the German guns, and the nurses revelled in it. I used to visit them frequently, and still retain vivid memories of wounded men being carried in on stretchers, with that terrible grey tinge to their faces, which always meant a very severe wound. The stretcher would be placed on a table in the operating tent, and the soldier would open his eyes. Then came the look of astonishment and joy when he saw a Sister or Nurse, and I used to feel that their mere presence meant that the wounded man was already half way to recovery.

At one stage during the Battle of Arnhem, when the Germans had succeeded in cutting our road to the rear, I visited our CCS which was established in a Dutch school in Nijmegen. As I stood in one of the wards, talking to the Head Sister, I heard the noise of a large enemy shell approaching. After a time in war, one gets to know instinctively whether or not an approaching shell is likely to land nearby. This one, I could tell, was going to be very, very close indeed. I would dearly have liked to take cover under one of the beds, but as the Sister seemed quite unmoved, I felt I had to grin and bear it. Then came a resounding crash, and all the windows were blown in. The Sister never even blinked. She finished what she was saying, then looked round and merely said, 'What a bore – we shall have to get all that repaired'. She did not know the meaning of the word fear, but had the gentlest of touches when it came to tending a wounded soldier.

She was, in fact, typical of the QAs and I cannot pay her a higher compliment than that.

CHAPTER 1

The Origins of Army Nursing

IT was a paper birth. Much thought, discussion and a great deal of paperwork preceded it. There were no parades or ceremonies to mark the day, no drumhead service. The date was 1 February, 1949, and the words on the paper read thus: '*Royal Warrant*. Formation of Queen Alexandra's Royal Army Nursing Corps.

'Whereas We deem it expedient to authorize with effect from 1 February, 1949, the formation of a corps to be entitled Queen Alexandra's Royal Army Nursing Corps, Our Will and Pleasure is that Queen Alexandra's Royal Army Nursing Corps shall be deemed a Corps for the purposes of the Army Act, the Reserve Forces Act, . . . rates of pay and conditions of service at present provided for officers of the Queen Alexandra's Imperial Military Nursing Service shall be applied to officers of the Queen Alexandra's Royal Army Nursing Corps until Our further Will and Pleasure be made known.'

It was signed by King George VI and Emanuel Shinwell, the Secretary of State for War, on 31 January, 1949.

Queen Alexandra's Imperial Military Nursing Service had not simply changed its name, it had become part of the British Army. Those in the new Corps were no longer merely attached to the army; they had become an integral part of the army itself. The nurses were transformed on that day into women soldiers and thereafter belonged to the senior women's corps in the army. How much difference it was to make to the individual nurses no one that day could tell. They continued, as they had been trained to do, to tend their patients – and 1 February, 1949 was just another day in military hospitals at home and over-seas.

On the same day the Auxiliary Territorial Service became the Women's Royal Army Corps, with the QARANC as the elder, sister corps. This was not a casual decision; their predecessors, after all, had been at the Crimea.

But the story leading up to the paper birthday started long before the battles of Alma, Balaclava and Inkerman, long before the wounded in the hospitals at Scutari, traditionally the birthplace of army nursing, received nursing help in 1854.

The earliest traces of organized army nursing in this country go back to the Roman occupation in AD 43, for it is known that the armies of the Roman Empire had military hospitals to care for their wounded. Some of these were in large houses and some were tented, a situation frequently repeated in later centuries.

The advent of Christianity had a direct effect on the military hospitals of the Roman Empire, for in AD 335 the Emperor Constantine, the first Christian Emperor, closed them down. This seemingly incongruous decision was taken because in that year Christianity became the state religion of Rome and the military hospitals were pagan institutions. Hitherto there had been no civilian hospitals within the Roman Empire.

The women workers in the early Christian Church, called deaconesses, were really the first nurses (one might also call them parish or social workers) and they, as those who were to follow them, regarded the caring for the sick as a vocation ordained by God. Indeed these early deaconesses, or 'nurses', were ordained by bishops. They had to be widowed or unmarried in order to become deaconesses and, as with all converts to Christianity in those infant days of the Church, they considered it to be both their pleasure and their duty to care for the poor, the sick and the bereaved.

It is fashionable nowadays to refer to nurses as members of a 'caring profession'. This tradition began in the days of Christian Rome and it was from those early Christian women that it was handed down the generations until, ironically, eighteen hundred years later it received the stimulus needed to become a profession through the work of an Englishwoman of Christian upbringing working in military hospitals in what had been the fringe of the Roman Empire.

The story of civilian nurses and nursing belongs to another

place but necessarily it must overlap with that of military nursing. Nevertheless, the overlapping during the centuries between the closure of Constantine's military hospitals and Florence Nightingale's work in Scutari was curiously limited.

The nursing activities of the deaconesses of the early Church ultimately spread, along with the Gospel they preached, to Britain. The hospitals of the fourth century AD housed not only the sick but orphans and the infirm as well, and since nursing duties were not confined to women, Christian men worked with the deaconesses, caring for the inmates.

The work of the deaconesses gradually became more and more monastic. Indeed Christianity was brought to Britain in AD 596 by St Augustine, a monk of the Order of St Benedict. The Augustinian Sisters are the oldest religious Community devoted solely to nursing. The Order was founded, under the Rule of St Augustine, in AD 650. Their hospital in Paris, the Hôtel-Dieu, was founded in 1443 and is believed to have been a model for many of the medieval hospitals in Britain.

While there is an obvious link between the two, the monastic tradition of nursing has a comparatively limited place in the story of military nursing. Nevertheless, to look ahead for a moment, it was at St Thomas's Hospital that Florence Nightingale founded her Training School for Nurses in 1860. That hospital, with St Bartholomew's and Bethlem Royal, is the oldest in Britain and when these three were founded the nursing staffs were all members of the Augustinian Order, both brothers and sisters. The term 'Sister', still in use in civil and military hospitals alike, derives from the monastic tradition when all skilled nursing was done by nuns.

'Leeches' went with Richard I's Crusaders to the Holy Land at the end of the twelfth century. The Knights of St John of Jerusalem, the militarily organized medical religious Order, sprang from that period, belonging as it did first to the Holy Land and then, when the Crusading days were over, to Rhodes and then to Malta. The historical connection between the Order and the QAs may be tenuous, but there are QAs now who recall that of the many RAMC orderlies called up for the War of

1939–45 whom they had to train, those who had served in peacetime with the St John Ambulance Brigade were among the more ready learners.

Ladies were allowed to join the Order of the Knights of St John and nursed the Crusaders in Palestine. One might call them forerunners of the QAs, for they were certainly among the earliest recognized military nurses.

By the time of the Crusades the pattern of women wanting, rather than having, to nurse men at arms had been established. As has been said, it is the most natural thing for any woman to want to nurse a sick or wounded man but until there was a regular army it was hardly possible to consistently nurse fighting men as such.

Edward I had surgeons attached to his armies in Scotland during the last two years of the thirteenth century and Edward II's surgeons also shaved the troops, which was logical since it was the 'chirurgeon's' trade which grew out of that of the barber's. Military hospitals were established in Ireland during Elizabeth I's campaign there, but there was no military hospital nursing in England until the Civil War of 1642.

CHAPTER 2

Early Nursing in the Regular Army

T HE Savoy Hospital in the Strand in London, the Hospital
of St John the Baptist, was founded in the sixteenth century.
Monks were the original nursing staff but it was not long
before there was a doctor there, and a matron and twelve secular
women, caring for the patients. In 1642, just over a hundred and
twenty years after its foundation, this hospital was emptied of all
those in its care, and the beds occupied by soldiers wounded in
the Civil War. The Committee for Maimed Soldiers organized
this transformation of a civil hospital into a purely military one.
Four of the women employed there were allowed to remain
and were referred to as nurses, and by the middle of the Civil
War their pay was five shillings a week. By the end of the
Civil War two other houses in London were also being used for
nursing the wounded. The Savoy Hospital remained open after
the war was over and continued to be used for sick and wounded
fighting men and to have a proportion of female nursing staff.

Of course St Thomas's, St Bartholomew's and Bethlem took
in casualties of the Civil War as well as the three 'military' hospitals. And homes near the battlefields were used to house the
wounded who were too ill to be taken to London.

The Commonwealth Army of Oliver Cromwell organized a
hospital for the wounded at Dunkirk during the Flanders
Campaign. Nuns tended the wounded there, but generally it was
a group of soldiers' wives who went with the troops overseas,
as, for instance, to the West Indies during the Spanish War of
1654–59 when Jamaica was captured from the Spaniards. The
regiments of Cromwell's Army each had their own surgeon and
surgeon's mates, and the women of the regiment nursed when
necessary. It was in the West Indies at that time that a hospital
ship was first used by Britain.

The Restoration of the Monarchy in 1660 gave the country a

regular army at last. Charles II wanted, indeed needed, it, but he had to act with care for there was a general dislike in the country for such an institution which the Cromwellian Army had done nothing to dispel. Charles II married Catharine of Braganza shortly after the Restoration and the port of Tangier, which had been a Portuguese possession for two hundred years, formed part of her dowry, as did the port of Bombay. Bombay belongs to a much later place in the story of military nursing. Tangier, however, does have an immediate connection.

The town had long been attacked by the Moors and therefore it had to be garrisoned. The King found no difficulty in raising a regiment for the defence of his new possession, in spite of the antipathy towards a standing army at home. The new regiment was raised in 1661, and was first known as the Tangier Regiment. Later it became The Queen's Regiment, after the Queen Consort.

By 1675 the regiment had its own hospital in Tangier which served the town as well as the soldiers. It was staffed by a 'Phisitian, a Chirurgeon and a Chirurgeon's Mate'. More recruits for the regiment came out in 1677 and among them 'two . . . women in men's clothes'. It is not revealed whether these women were called upon to work in the hospital when their sex was discovered, but it is known that when the ships mustered off Cadiz and Tangier for the final evacuation in 1684 there was among them a hospital ship, *Welcome*, with a Dr Lawrence in charge of forty sick soldiers and seamen and 'women for nurses: 2'. *Welcome* was the only hospital ship in the convoy, the two women on board who acted as nurses were among the earliest to care for the British Army at sea.

Charles II's regular army inevitably brought regular army medicine into being, in that military doctors were granted regular commissions. Those in regiments had a lowly status even though they ran the small regimental hospitals, but at least they were there and the idea of tending the needs of the sick and wounded soldiery of the permanent army had arrived.

The Commissioners for Sick and Wounded Seamen and Soldiers and Prisoners worked at home during the wars with the Dutch, which had begun before the Restoration and were to continue until 1667, and arranged for beds in St Thomas's Hospital to be reserved for casualties. Emergency hospitals were also set up in some English coastal towns, with women employed as nurses.

James II arranged for army hospitals to be set up on Hounslow Heath. Each had a matron and female servants to help with the nursing, cooking and washing, but only during the summer season. However, the care of the soldiery was still primitive and cheaply organized and the idea of women being regularly used as nurses in the army did not become established during the seventeenth and eighteenth centuries. Although, in 1742, there were hospitals in Flanders staffed by matrons with nurses and tenders under them and women did act as nurses during the fighting in North America in 1757 and in Spain in 1762, on the whole military nursing was haphazard and inefficient during the seventeenth and eighteenth centuries and remained so until well into the nineteenth, in spite of the efforts of Dr Monro.

Donald Monro, Physician to George III's army, wrote an account of the diseases most prevalent in the military hospitals in Germany between 1761 and 1763 at the end of the Seven Years War. In it he stated that every large Military Hospital should have a Head Nurse and sufficient nurses to care for the sick. He also wrote that the Matron or Head Nurse should go round the wards at least twice a day, seeing to it that they were clean and the nurses sober, and that they were to report anything amiss to a Physician, Surgeon or Apothecary.

As for the 'common nurses', Dr Monro considered it essential that they should keep the patients as neat and clean 'as the nature of their distempers will admit of', tell the Ward Master or Head Nurse of any deaths and take care of the clothes and effects of the deceased. Wards should be sprinkled with vinegar and fumigated with wetted gunpowder or Frankincense and windows should be opened once or twice a day, depending on the weather. He stressed the importance of fresh air and cleanliness, laying down that 'nastiness of any kind' was not to be thrown out of the open windows, that 'common necessaries' should be carried and that chamber pots and close-stools should be emptied, washed and returned as soon as used. Meat and 'spiritous liquors or other things of that kind' were not to be brought into the hospitals by the 'common nurses' unless allowed by the Physician. He concluded his instructions thus: 'Nurses guilty of great neglect of duty, or of getting drunk and using their patients ill, or of stealing or concealing or taking away the effects of men who die in the hospital, are to be immediately sent to the Guard, and reported to the Commanding Officer . . . that they may be tried by Court Martial, and be confined, whipped, or other-wise punished as the Military Law directs, all followers of Armies on foreign service being equally subject to Military Law as the soldiers themselves.'

The fact that it was necessary for Dr Monro to write in this way at that time shows that the quality of military nursing was not very high, but at least a standard was being postulated.

That a proportion of the nurses or 'followers' of the army in the mid-eighteenth century acted in another capacity as well as nursing, as doubtless women employed to nurse had done before them, and would continue to do, is most probable. The image of the nurse, as opposed to the religious nursing sister, was not then remotely like the image which was to develop in the latter part of the nineteenth century. But the women who did act as nurses for the army cannot be blamed for that. Nursing was not a profession. Indeed it was not to become one in the strictly legal sense in Britain until the twentieth century, when, in 1919, the word 'nurse' became protected in law.

By the end of the eighteenth century it was established that when a regiment was in barracks, a regimental hospital was to be founded and if a regiment consisted of five hundred men or more a 'nurse' was to be provided, together with a sergeant and an orderly. Nothing is known of the qualifications required of the nurse, but her duties were surely appreciated for her pay was a shilling a day, while the sergeant received only half that amount and the orderly fourpence. But this was hardly regular employment for the nurse, for if the regiment moved out of barracks or was divided up her services were no longer required and an orderly, or orderlies, replaced her.

1. *Miss Nightingale.*

2. *A drawing by E. Duncan of the Royal Victoria Military Hospital, Netley, near Southampton in 1863. 'The façade of the hospital was grand indeed.'*

3. *Florence Nightingale at Scutari: a painting entitled 'The Ministering Angel of the Crimean War' by Jerry Barrett and Samuel Bellini.*

4. *Nursing sisters, on active service during the Boer War, unpacking in South Africa.*

5. *An Army Nursing Sister accompanying a patient to hospital in South Africa.*

6. *A drawing by S. Begg of the Herbert Hospital, Woolwich. Queen Victoria went there in March, 1900, in a wheelchair (distributing posies from Frogmore to the patients in the two surgical wards she visited). The Nursing Sister is wearing the badge of Princess Christian's Army Nursing Service Reserve.*

As well as the regimental hospitals there were a few General Military Hospitals in the United Kingdom, but the employment of female nursing staff was not encouraged; even the Royal Artillery Hospital at Woolwich had, apart from a Head Nurse, only one nurse to every three wards.

By 1800 Matrons (at two shillings and sixpence a day) and Head Nurses were employed in regimental hospitals, but as late as 1838 the instructions concerning their engagement and duties (instructions first issued in 1812) read: 'Preference should be given to the wife of an NCO or soldier of the Regiment'. The regimental nurses were supposed to be 'sober, careful, cleanly and . . . accustomed to the charge and management of sick persons'. Possibly many of the wives of the regiments did have those qualities and experience. It is also certain that many did not, although through practice probably some of them acquired certain nursing skills.

Wellington's army in the Peninsular Wars had no nurses as such. Nurses in civil hospitals at home were notorious for their promiscuity and their drunkenness and probably this contributed to Wellington's efforts to reduce the wagon trains of camp followers. Among the women with Wellington's army there were, of course, soldiers' wives who did fine work nursing their husbands and their comrades as well. This they did under appalling conditions, as described in contemporary accounts such as that of Rifleman Harris. The women had the greatest difficulty in keeping up with an army constantly on the move, and it is understandable that they were regarded as impedimenta rather than as being of practical help to the sick and wounded. One can but pity those women who on occasion had to bury their husbands as well as try and nurse them without proper provision being made for their transport, let alone comfort. Venereal and other diseases riddled the army and the plight of the women with it was often as hard as it was for the wounded whom they tried to nurse.

CHAPTER 3

Miss Nightingale and the Crimean War

WHEN Britain and France declared war on Russia in 1854 the medical arrangements in the army were in a deplorable state of neglect. When the British army was sent to the Crimea there were no trained stretcher bearers, no ambulance transport and no proper organization for the supply of food and equipment, let alone medical supplies. The army arrived in the summer. By the time Florence Nightingale reached the Barrack Hospital at Scutari on 4 November, having left England on 21 October, she found the quarters reserved for her party of nurses to be without furniture, cleaning materials and medical supplies. There was an allowance of water of a pint a day, for both washing and drinking. There was also the corpse of a Russian General in the room in which some of the nurses were to sleep.

The events which led up to the arrival of Florence Nightingale, in the Crimea are almost too well known to bear repetition. Briefly, William Howard Russell of *The Times* wrote, in early October 1854, of the conditions existing in the Barrack Hospital at Scutari. The public learned that those wounded at the Battle of the Alma had no dressers or nurses, no bandages and that the sick and wounded had to lie on the filth-covered floor. At that time the army was jointly administered by the Secretary at War and the Secretary for War. Financial administration came under the jurisdiction of the former and the fact that the Medical Services were incapable of dealing with the casualties during the early part of the Crimean War was partly due to the economies which had long been practised by the Secretary at War's department. The holder of that office in 1854 (appointed in 1852) was Sidney Herbert. He read Russell's dispatches and acted. One of his actions was to write to Florence Nightingale and ask her to go to the Crimea with a party of nurses to organize and superintend the nursing in the hospitals in Scutari. His letter crossed with one from her to Mrs Herbert in which she volunteered to go in just such a capacity and asked whether Mr Herbert would approve.

Florence Nightingale's qualifications were unique. Born into a family of gentle birth five years after the Battle of Waterloo, in 1849 she broke away from the conventional social *mores* of the day by going to the Lutheran Kaiserwerth Institution of Deaconesses in Germany to study hospital nursing at first hand. She stayed a fortnight. Two years later she returned for a few months, working in the hospital – the Institution included an orphanage and school as well as a training school for teachers – and adding practical experience to her knowledge of hygiene, which she had already studied on her own. She was an industrious, highly intelligent and religious young woman who had long wanted to nurse. In the case of Florence Nightingale it can truly be said that she had a vocation.

In the two years following her return from Kaiserswerth she continued to study, in spite of family pressures, and learned much about sanitation, hospital nursing and administration and hygiene. She also visited the Hospital of the Sisters of Mercy in Paris. She had intended to nurse and study there, but her family sent for her to look after her ill grandmother. Her clarity of vision and organizational ability, as well as her sense of vocation, were becoming well known and in 1853 she was put in charge of a nursing home for 'Gentlewomen during Illness' in Harley Street. The following year she superintended the nursing, in a voluntary capacity, at the Middlesex Hospital during the cholera outbreak of that summer. Two months later she was on her way to Scutari.

Sidney Herbert gave her every encouragement both before she went and while she was there; indeed he asked her to report to him privately on the conditions she found in the hospitals to which she was sent. With typical efficiency, she assembled a group of women to accompany her. It was not easy to find suitable volunteers. She was insistent that a uniform was to be worn, although those in religious orders wore their habits, and that her own orders were to be obeyed implicitly. Miss Nightingale's nurses wore long black dresses with white collars and a linen band reaching from the right shoulder to the left side of the waist with the words 'Scutari Hospital' embroidered in red upon it. Instant dismissal was to be the punishment for misconduct with the troops. In the end she was only able to gather a party of thirty-eight, of whom ten were Roman Catholic nuns (who had to submit to taking orders regarding nursing from Miss Nightingale rather than from their Mother Superior), fourteen were lay nurses from civil hospitals, six were from a High Church Sisterhood, and eight from the Sellonites.

The Sellonites took their name from their foundress, Priscilla Lydia Sellon, who had started 'The Church of England Sisterhood of Mercy of Devonport and Plymouth' in 1848, before Florence Nightingale's concern for the care of the sick was known to the public. The Sisterhood had had much experience of nursing cholera in Plymouth in 1849 and again in 1853. Their experience was to help them in their endeavours at the Barrack Hospital, for an outbreak of cholera occurred within a month of their arrival.

Florence Nightingale's party sailed from Marseilles on 27 October, 1854 – having travelled overland from Boulogne – in a cockroach-ridden vessel, the *Vectis*. Before leaving France Miss Nightingale bought provisions and portable stoves; they were to be much needed. They reached Scutari ten days after the Battle of Balaclava and on the eve of the Battle of Inkerman.

The hospital catering arrangements were almost non-existent. There was only one kitchen and large coppers were the only cooking utensils; tea was made and meat was boiled (when the water did boil) in them. Miss Nightingale's work for the sick soldiery started when the medical authorities gave permission for her nurses to provide pails of arrowroot and wine for the patients. The kitchen in her own quarters then became the diet kitchen of the hospital. For, while Florence Nightingale succeeded in bringing order out of chaos, it must be remembered that she did so within the rules obtaining and not by breaking them. Even in the provision of invalid diets to the sufferers from cholera and dysentry, nothing was allowed to leave her kitchen unless a requisition signed by a doctor was produced.

It had been Sidney Herbert's intention to give Florence Nightingale overall powers. Her title was 'Superintendent of the Female Nursing Establishment of the English General Military Hospitals in Turkey'. That should have been explicit enough. Scutari, on the eastern shore of the Bosphorus, facing Constantinople, was indeed in Turkey. Balaclava, however, was not; it was in the Crimea, and separated from Turkey by 300 miles of the Black Sea. It was hard indeed that when her administrative skill had so improved conditions in the Barrack Hospital in Scutari that she felt able to go to the Crimea to visit the hospitals there, she should not only become seriously ill with 'Crimean Fever', but have her authority challenged by at least one doctor. He was Dr John Hall, Chief of Medical Staff of the British Expeditionary Army. He directed his antagonism towards her, which was surely really jealousy, by drawing attention to the word 'Turkey' in her title. She nevertheless overcame both illness and the active non-co-operation of Dr Hall and certain other doctors and continued her work of succouring the sick and wounded.

Her influence in the war area and at home was great, and she used it for the benefit of the troops. There is only one recorded instance of her having used it for the betterment of her friends, and even that was done for the eventual good of the patients. She asked Sidney Herbert to cause Dr McGrigor to be promoted two years before Regulations would have normally allowed and so perform 'a service to humanity at the expense of the Regulations of the Service'. Sidney Herbert did as he was bidden.

In 1855 Lord Aberdeen's Government fell and Lord Palmerston, another of Florence Nightingale's influential friends, became Prime Minister. The offices of Secretary at War and Secretary for War were combined and given to Lord Panmure. He was told to pay heed to Miss Nightingale and so he did. He caused a Sanitary Commission to be sent out to the Crimea; an action of which she greatly approved, later saying that it 'saved the British Army'.

Florence Nightingale's activities in the Crimean War are remembered for two reasons. The first was her brilliant use of her talent for rationalization. Working as she did within the existing organization, by scrupulous attention to detail, she achieved order where previously there had been none. She wrote an incredible number of reports and letters. This in itself was a physical hardship, as she suffered much from cold and fatigue in order to keep ahead of the office work, all of which she had to do in her bedroom. She attended to the provision of proper food for the patients, with the invaluable help of a French chef named Alexis Soyer. She kept discipline among her nurses. This, too, was a formidable undertaking, since several of the lay members of her team were prone to drunkenness. She opened a reading room for convalescent men, as well as recreation rooms, schools and singing classes. No recreational activities of any kind had hitherto been provided; the only solace from boredom was drink. She even sent money from soldiers' pay home at their request.

With all this organizational work one would imagine that she would have been more than fully occupied. Nevertheless, she is also remembered for her actual nursing of the patients. On one occasion she personally nursed for twenty-four hours without respite as casualties poured into the Barrack Hospital, and more than one instance is recorded of her spending up to eight hours on her knees, dressing wounds. She made night rounds (and it was estimated there were four miles of beds there), comforting, encouraging and soothing. No wonder the troops 'kissed her shadow' as she passed. 'The Lady with the Lamp' may have been feared by Authority, but she was loved by the soldiers and she loved them.

When the war was over a fund was raised to commemorate Florence Nightingale's work in the Crimea. It was known as the Nightingale Fund and, at her request, it was used to found the Nightingale School of Nursing at St Thomas's Hospital. This was the first such institution in England and there were initially fifteen pupils. The first Superintendent was Mrs Wardroper, Matron of St Thomas's. The initial step toward professionalism had been taken and, with Sarah Anne Terrot, who had served in the Crimea with the Sellonites, as Assistant to Mrs Wardroper, civilian and military nurses took the step together.

CHAPTER 4

A System is Established

FLORENCE NIGHTINGALE'S concern with the welfare of the British soldier did not end with the Crimean War and her return to England in 1856. Typically, she stayed in the Crimea until the last soldier had been discharged from hospital. While it is true that Rudyard Kipling immortalized Tommy Atkins, it is surely equally true to say that Florence Nightingale discovered him. She recognized in Tommy Atkins a man capable of courage and endurance, of initiative and compassion, a man who had often been considered to be expendable by his officers and the public, a man subject to fear (and he had much to fear in hospital in those days before anaesthetic and disinfectant), a man responsive to care, encouragement and leadership. She recognized Tommy Atkins to be a worthwhile human being and she directed her talents and her compassion to his well-being when both returned from the war.

With her old friend Sidney Herbert she planned and worked for the Royal Commission on the Health of the Army and worked on the Royal Sanitary Commission on the Health of the Army in India. She gave advice over the Egyptian Campaign in 1884. Indeed she personally selected the nurses who went on the expedition to relieve Gen Gordon. And she wrote, among much other material, *Notes on Matters Affecting the Health, Efficiency, and Hospital Administration of the British Army.*

Although never part of the War Office, she worked with it and advised it. She referred to the rooms in London where she lived as 'the little War Office', and, although a sick woman, the amount of work she did for the army, for nursing and for sanitation in India and at home, was prodigious. As far as the army was concerned, it was as though, while not actually part of it, she considered its welfare to be part of herself.

Apart from all the work connected with the Royal Commission, Florence Nightingale involved herself with the new military hospital to be built on Southampton Water at Netley, approximately twelve miles from Portsmouth and six from Southampton.

Queen Victoria, whose somewhat sentimental compassion for her troops was well known, admired Florence Nightingale and her work greatly. They had met for the first time on 21 September, 1856 at Balmoral, when Miss Nightingale told her much of the sufferings the soldiers had endured in the Crimea. In the same year the Queen laid the foundation stone of the military hospital at Netley, designed by a War Department architect named Mennie to accommodate 'sick and wounded soldiers of Queen Victoria's Army'.

It was her first official act following the end of the Crimean War and she arrived in the Royal Yacht, escorted by gunboats, to perform it. The Queen landed on a specially built wooden jetty covered in scarlet cloth. A salute was fired by the gunboats when the stone was laid. Unfortunately one gun went off too soon and two seamen were killed instantly and others injured. However, the ceremony continued.

One hundred and ten years after the stone was laid it was lifted, two and a half tons of Welsh granite, and underneath was found a smaller piece of Bath stone inscribed 'Victoria Military Hospital, 1856'. When this second stone was raised a copper casket was revealed. This was opened by the officer commanding the Royal Victoria Hospital, as Netley had by that time become, and found to contain a set of coins (including a groat and a crown) of the year 1853. They were, in all probability, a proof set. No such sets were minted between 1854 and 1856, which accounts for the coins being dated three years before they were placed under the foundation stone of Netley. The casket also contained another anachronism: a Victoria Cross. This, the highest award for gallantry in the field, was not instituted until 1857, and the medal in the casket is thought to have been a prototype given to the Queen. There was another medal as well: the Crimea Medal, with the four clasps of Sebastopol, Inkerman, Balaklava and Alma. That was singularly appropriate: the war had given rise to the new concern for the welfare of the British soldier and the new military hospital was a part of that concern. The casket also contained the plans of the building.

Florence Nightingale's *Notes on Matters Affecting the Health, Efficiency, and Hospital Administration of the British Army* and *Subsidiary Notes as to the Introduction of Female Nursing into Military Hospitals in Peace and in War* were not published until two years after the foundation stone had been laid and five years before the hospital admitted the first patients on 19 May, 1863. However, she knew more than any other living person about the care of soldiers in hospital and she thoroughly disapproved of the plans. More than that, she tried very hard indeed to have them altered, appealing both to Lord Panmure and to the Prime Minister, Lord Palmerston. Her efforts were of no avail; building had already begun and it would have cost £70,000 to pull it down and begin again. So it was not Florence Nightingale's fault that no sunlight came into the wards, which faced north-east and overlooked the coal heaps and outhouses behind the hospital, nor that there was scant provision for the circulation of fresh air or for isolation units.

The façade of the hospital was grand indeed. It looked over Southampton Water and was outwardly admired by many, but from inside the view could only be enjoyed by those in the administrative block. It was a brick building set in two hundred and twenty-seven acres of grounds, with Portland stone dressings and an attenuated dome in the centre, between two wings. It measured 1,424 feet in length and corridors on the three floors, overlooking the grounds and Southampton Water, extended from one end to the other. During the Second World War, when Netley was used by the American Army, jeeps were used on the ground floor to travel the distance of over a quarter of a mile.

The hospital had its own water and lighting supply. It also had, and has still, its own beautifully kept cemetery. It possessed its own railway station as well, with a line connecting it to Southampton Central Station. That private railway was built seventeen years before the Portsmouth Line, so highly did the authorities

c

regard the importance of Netley, reputed to be the largest military hospital in the world.

Miss Nightingale, however, viewed it with disfavour; the care and comfort of the British soldier meant far more to her than the grandiose structure, which was only to last for just over a hundred years. When the time came on 16 September, 1966 to pull it down, it proved to be one of the largest demolition jobs ever undertaken. It did, however, play an important part in the story of military nursing.

The Army Medical School (another project dear to Florence Nightingale and owing much to her) came into being in 1860 at Fort Pitt in Chatham and moved to the Royal Victoria Hospital in 1863, the year the first patients arrived; it was to remain at Netley for forty years. When the Army Nursing Service came into being in 1881, Netley was its Headquarters and Depot. Indeed, Netley has been called the cradle of the Army Nursing Service.

Many hundreds of British, American and Empire soldiers, have been nursed there. The old hospital building finally became empty in 1958. Pipes froze and burst in the cold winter of 1963, causing much damage and later that year the building was further damaged by fire. Now all that remains is the Royal Chapel. But the work of the hospital is carried on in the buildings erected during the Second World War behind the original hospital, and this comparatively new Royal Victoria Hospital is used by the three Services. The Officers' Mess at Royal Victoria Hospital, Netley was the first in the United Kingdom to be used both by the Royal Navy and the Army.

The exact date of the opening of the Herbert Hospital at Woolwich is not known, but it was certainly completed by 1866 and the centenary celebrations took place on 12 November, 1965. This time Florence Nightingale did approve and, with Sidney Herbert, had much to do with its design and construction. It was she who insisted that it should bear his name. He had died in 1861, having become Lord Herbert of Lea early in the same year.

Whereas Netley was of the old 'corridor' type, the Herbert and, later, the Cambridge, were built to Miss Nightingale's 'pavilion' specifications with airy wards and plenty of sunlight.

The first Governor of the hospital, Col Shaw, took up his appointment on 1 November, 1865. There were a few female nurses working at the old garrison hospital in Woolwich when Col Shaw became Governor, but there were none at the Herbert. However, Mrs Shaw Stewart (who had been in the Crimea with Florence Nightingale) and eight attendant lady nurses soon took up day duty. They had quarters in the Female Infirmary in Woolwich. In October of the following year *The Times* carried the following report: 'It was stated yesterday (the 16th) that the number of patients in the Herbert Hospital amounted to about three hundred, and that nineteen in twenty had been understood to have expressed a dislike to the attendance of female nurses being thrust upon them contrary to their desire.'

The Herbert had been planned to accommodate six hundred and forty beds and in those early days one female nurse was allocated to each ward (except the venereal and convalescent wards); no nurse had less than twenty-five patients.

It is not known when the Herbert was given the prefix 'Royal'. In March 1900 Queen Victoria went there in a wheelchair, distributing posies from Frogmore to the patients in the two surgical wards she visited, and it has been assumed that that was the year in which the hospital became the Royal Herbert. However, an invitation card sent out on the occasion of the visit of King Edward VII and Queen Alexandra on 16 February, 1903, does not carry the prefix and the Court Circular issued from Buckingham Palace on that date refers to the visit as being to the Herbert Hospital.

The third large military hospital to be built was the Cambridge in Aldershot. Named after the Duke of Cambridge, it was opened by him in July 1879. It was, like the Herbert, built on 'Nightingale' lines. The plans had been presented to the House of Commons as long before as 1858 and it is worth noting that the interior walls of the wards were to be plastered, as at Netley, and not just whitewashed as had been customary hitherto.

In 1898 another hospital was opened in Aldershot for the sole purpose of caring for the wives and children of the army. Princess Louise Margaret, Duchess of Connaught, performed the inauguration ceremony and the hospital bears her name. The Duke of Connaught was GOC Aldershot Command at the time. The fact that it was purpose built is evidenced by the shallow staircases: the nurses could run up and down them quickly in the long dresses of the period.

The Louise Margaret remained a general hospital for women and children until 1958, when it became the Louise Margaret Maternity Hospital. It is now, as all the other military hospitals, a teaching hospital and is approved by the Central Midwives Board as a training school for pupil midwives, as well as being recognized by the Royal College of Obstetricians and Gynaecologists as a training place for Medical Officers intent on becoming Specialist Obstetricians.

In February 1880, Sir William Muir, who was then Director General of the Army Medical Department, received a letter from the National Society for Aid to the Sick and Wounded in War, which had come into being in 1870 following the outbreak of the Franco-Prussian War. Florence Nightingale was a member of the Ladies' Committee of which Princess Christian of Schleswig-Holstein was Chairman. The letter said that the Executive Committee had sanctioned an annual grant 'for the purpose of training and maintaining a Staff of Nurses . . . amounting to £1,100 per annum'. The Secretary of State for War was also informed of this decision, and the letter went on to say: 'The National Society's chief object is to provide the means of training a certain number of nurses at Netley and subsequently maintaining them at the other Military Hospitals, whose services may afterwards be available in case of War. The length of the period of their training and work will be left to your discretion but in order to ensure the training of a succession of nurses it will probably be desirable to assign a limited period – say from two to three years for the curriculum.'

By June of that year Mrs Jane C. Deeble had become the first Superintendent of Nurses at the Royal Victoria Hospital, Netley.

She had then been there eleven years, having first gone as one of six Sisters from St Thomas's, where she had completed her training. There was not enough room in June 1880 to take in extra nurses, but by October accommodation was ready and Mrs Deeble asked the Government for six sets of furniture. Among the sets of furniture which Mrs Deeble obtained for their use were Soiled Linen Baskets, Clothes Presses, Large Water Cans and Small Foot Baths.

It was arranged that the training of these nurses would be performed under the auspices of the National Society, and that they would serve on probation for a year, after one month's trial. A period of two years in a military hospital would follow, during which time they would be paid (by the National Society) thirty pounds a year. During the trial and probation time their pay was to be twelve pounds. On 1 January, 1881 Mrs Deeble approved the following advertisement 'for insertion in a *few* papers':

'NURSING SISTERS: Arrangements having been made for a limited number of Nursing Sisters to be trained in military hospitals under the auspices of the National Society for Aid to the Sick and Wounded in War, Candidates are hereby informed that particular information regarding these appointments can be obtained by application to Mrs Deeble, Superintendent of Nurses, Netley. Preference will be given to widows and daughters of officers of H.M.'s Services.'

The notice appeared in *The Times* and the *Daily Telegraph*. By May 1881, the ladies had been chosen, only one of whom was a widow. Their uniform included two grey dresses, a straw hat, a winter and summer cloak and, of course, aprons. 1881 was the year in which the Army Nursing Service officially came into being, with Mrs Deeble as Lady Superintendent, although by that time the principle as well as the fact that the Army needed its own trained women nurses both at home and overseas was well established, fourteen nurses under Mrs Deeble having gone from Netley for service in the Zulu War in 1879. Eight of these were sent to Pietermaritzburg, but Mrs Deeble and the rest went to the township of Addington, where a hospital had been built in 1878. When the war between Natal and the Zulu King, Cetshwayo, broke out, it was commandeered by the Government for the wounded. The last inmates were moved to another hospital at the end of 1879.

Not unnaturally the National Society asked for details of the training of their nurses and Mrs Deeble sent them, via the Army Medical Department, at the beginning of August 1881. It was a comprehensive curriculum, and from it we learn much about the life of the nurses in training. They got up at 6.30 each morning and went to bed at 10 o'clock. Their day was a full one: they were in the wards from 8 am until 1 pm. Time was allocated for exercise and prayer (half an hour being provided for the latter), and they were taught, among other things, how to dress blisters, wounds and bedsores, the application of leeches and dry cupping, the administration of medicines and enemas, the names and uses of surgical implements, strict observation of the sick and so on.

In the following May the probationers all took written, oral and practical examinations, which each one of them passed. They proved their knowledge of such things as bandaging and of surgical instruments, which might have to be used before the arrival of a surgeon, in the practical examination, and successfully answered questions ranging from the most obvious signs of death and symptoms of enteric and typhoid fevers to 'what points require attention in application of leeches?'

Of these particular nurses it is known that two of them served in Egypt in 1884 during the attempt to relieve Gen Gordon at Khartoum, and three of them transferred permanently to the Army Nursing Service after their period of service under the auspices of the National Society. Twelve nurses trained under this scheme and in 1885 it came to an end, the National Society saying they could lend no more nurses, other than those already under training at Netley.

In 1882 Florence Nightingale wrote the famous message to the Army Nurses on the eve of their departure to the Middle East for the Egyptian Campaign. She had visited Egypt once herself, in 1849, while recuperating from an illness, but had never been back. She said: 'Remember when you are far away up country, possibly the only Englishwoman there, that these men will note and remember your every action, not only as a nurse but as a woman: your life to them will be as the rings a pebble makes when thrown into a pond – reaching far and reaching wide, each ripple gone beyond our grasp, yet remembered almost to exaggeration by these soldiers lying helpless in their sickness. See that your every word and act is worthy of your profession and your womanhood. God guard you in His safekeeping and make you worthy of His trust – our soldiers.'

She had set the standard herself in the Crimea; it was a standard which was to be maintained.

Nurses of the Army Nursing Service served in the Sudan War of 1883–84. They nursed in the Citadel in Cairo as well as aboard hospital ships up and down the Nile. Indeed it is said that the first white women to go up the Nile were army nurses. During the Nile Campaign of 1889 two nursing sisters, with an Egyptian coolie servant, went from Cairo to Assouan – First Cataract by boat during the Battle of Toski. That journey, the river being low, took nine days. After the battle the return journey took only five days. The temperature during that period was 116°. The ladies must have been uncomfortable indeed, for while they were ashore they slept in a mud hut. It had two openings, one a 'window' and the other a 'door'. The 'door' had a blanket across it and the servant slept outside it to stop 'wild beasts', as one of the pair described them, coming in during the night. Adaptability, or resourcefulness, is an essential quality of the good nurse, and undoubtedly those early members of the Army Nursing Service had it.

In England by 1883, when the Army Nursing Service was but two years old and the Louise Margaret had yet to be built, the days of Mrs Gamp and drunken civilian nurses were passing. Nurses in civil hospitals were living down their pre-Nightingale past and the War Office sufficiently recognized the value of women nurses abroad as well as at home to decree that Sisters were to be employed in all army hospitals of a hundred beds or more. The Netley-trained ladies were gradually to be found not only at the Herbert and the Cambridge but at hospitals in

Gosport, Portsmouth, Devonport, Dover, Shorncliffe and Canter-bury. They also went across the Irish Sea to the Curragh and to the Mediterranean bases at Malta and Gibraltar.

An Army Hospital Services Inquiry Commission was held in January of that year at the War Office in Pall Mall. Mrs Deeble went to London from Netley to give evidence and Miss A. E. Caulfeild, Superintendent of Nurses at the Herbert Hospital, travelled from Woolwich. The Minutes inform us of the duties expected of the 'considerable staff of nursing sisters' by Miss Caulfeild and that her Sisters generally had two orderlies in each ward to work under their direction. Orderlies apparently worked better under the Sisters than on their own. She confirmed Mrs Deeble's statement that Sisters were, at that time, employed only at the Herbert and at Netley, (There were, of course, a few Sisters in Egypt with the army.) and that if Sisters were to be employed at other military hospitals not less than four or five should go. 'I should not care to send one or two women alone to live in a hospital.' She stated further that in her view it was most important that the Sisters in 'Her Majesty's Nursing Service' should be good nurses and that the widows or daughters of officers would be the most suitable 'rank' from which the Sisters should be drawn. While she thought that the wives of soldiers would be 'too much on a level with the men themselves', she also said that, although it would be preferable to have only ladies in the Service, this was not possible and 'if you get a really good nurse, a good sensible woman, I do not see that the question of social rank should be a drawback'. She added that the nurses had all had experience in civil hospitals before going to Netley but that she thought, 'the idea was that the National Aid Sisters were to be trained at Netley. A few have been trained at civil hospitals, but the majority of them, I think, have been trained at Netley; and the idea was to train them in a military hospital without any civil training.'

When making this statement – which in a sense was prophetic – Miss Caulfeild had already pointed out that in a civil hospital the patients were nearly all in beds, whereas in a military hos-pital in peacetime there would be only a few men in beds in each ward, 'the others walking about with slight ailments'. Hence the desirability for the Sisters to have had civil hospital experience.

Miss Caulfeild finished her evidence with a plea for 'some fixed rules regarding pensions for the Sisters', since the extension of female nursing in the Army was under consideration, as 'it would be an inducement to many good women to stay in the Service'.

Mrs Deeble described the duties of the Nursing Sisters at Netley thus: 'They administer all the medicines, they do all the dressings [and] surgical dressings, they apply all the blisters and dry cups; in the medical division they administer all the morphia injections, they give the enemas, the nutritive enemas and the others, they do the sick cookery for the sick, prepare their drinks, beef-tea, puddings, etc.'

She went on to say that each Sister was provided with a little cooking stove of her own on which to do the cooking (Miss Caulfeild had said that the Sisters at the Herbert did very little cooking for the patients and that 'we never make beef-tea'), that the Sisters did more than in a civil hospital – 'It is a combined charge; they do the work of a nurse and a Sister together,' – and that 'they wash and generally take care of, and make up the beds of, the helpless cases'. She stressed that the orderlies 'do very little of the nursing'.

The Inquiry Committee raised with Mrs Deeble, as it had with Miss Caulfeild, the matter of the type of nurse required in military hospitals, to which she made this revealing and opinionated reply: 'A class of women entirely superior to that of the wardmaster and the sergeants, because she must be a terror to the wrongdoer. When a Sister comes it must be "Oh, here is Sister"; she should be the shadow of the medical officer, and she should be superior to all the female relations of the patients if she is to have her proper influence.'

From her evidence it is apparent that Mrs Deeble's husband had been a doctor who 'used to trust his hospital sergeant a great deal'. She considered that the Sisters should have a recognized rank in order to ensure discipline of the orderlies, and that orderlies should be taught to cook in the interest of the patients.

She said that at Netley each Sister had from sixty to seventy patients under her charge but that not all were confined to their beds. In her opinion, based on her own experiences in Africa during the Zulu War, stoves should be provided 'that would go round the pole of a tent'. Mrs Deeble always laid stress on the importance of ready nourishment for her soldier patients. She also stressed that if Sisters were to go to other military hospitals, three should be the minimum number and not less than five if they were to do night duty. She, like Miss Caulfeild, made a plea for pensions and higher pay.

Florence Nightingale kept in close touch with nurses both at home and abroad. For instance, in 1886 she wrote to 'The Acting Sister in Charge, Royal Victoria Hospital, Suez, Egypt', asking for news of one of the Sisters there, who was sick. The Acting Sister in Charge at that time was Ada Hind.

Miss Hind was later asked to form the Indian Army Nursing Service, but she declined owing to ill health, and it was Miss Loch and Miss Oxley who were selected by the India Office to inaugurate the use of skilled nurses in the military hospitals in India. Eight Nursing Sisters went to India in 1888, with Miss Loch and Miss Oxley as Lady Superintendents. They were to form the nucleus of the Indian Army Nursing Service. Miss Loch saw field service early in her career in India, for she and four Nursing Sisters went on the Black Mountain Expedition in North-West India that year. While in Abbottabad she wrote:

'Before leaving I made a sketch of the Black Mountain, as seen from our tents. Somehow there was a mistake, and our mounted escort never turned up: so we went on accompanied by only one native soldier and by a syce (groom) . . . We had our revolvers belted on and felt very warlike. However, we did not see the ghost of an enemy and got here safely . . . Darband is only 14 or 15 miles from Oghi [where she had been nursing under canvas], but there being no road over the mountains we have to go this roundabout way.'

She got there two days later, having waded across a wide river bed with streams in it, 'only one being more than knee-deep', having urged on her attendants who were fearful of robbers by showing them the revolver which she carried and having eaten native food when her own ran out.

Miss Loch's life in India – she was to become the Senior Lady Superintendent, Queen Alexandra's Military Nursing Service for India – was by no means all a series of adventures. She organized, she nursed, she travelled, she maintained discipline among her Sisters and, with them, met illnesses with which they had not been familiar before going to India, such as enteric fever.

A year after her arrival, she wrote: 'I have just been writing a long letter to Miss Nightingale in answer to one of hers. She does write such charming letters, full of encouragement and also lots of questions about our work.'

In the following year, 1890, while trying to get nominal rank for her Sisters assured, she wrote:

'And I have also felt most strongly the difference in the position of the military and the naval Sisters, whose rank* as Commissioned Officers is recognized and works perfectly. Besides the fact, which was strongly represented in the letters of appeal, that the Netley Sisters are not nearly so much exposed to difficulty as we are, for they only work in three or four central hospitals where they have been a recognized institution for years, and they work with the trained men of the Army Hospital Corps, while we are popped hither and thither, and even when stationary have incessantly new orderlies, men drawn at random from the ranks and generally chosen because they are little or no credit to the regiment and therefore are easier spared.'

This is a most revealing comment on military nursing of the time.

* Miss Loch presumably meant 'status'. Rank titles as such were not used in 1890. Naval Sisters always have been civilians attached to the Royal Navy, ever since the first Sisters were appointed to the Naval Hospital at Haslar in 1884.

CHAPTER 5

The South African War

IN 1897, the year of her mother's Diamond Jubilee, Queen
Victoria's third daughter and fifth child, Princess Christian
of Schleswig Holstein, first Chairman of the Ladies Committee
of the British Red Cross Society, started the Army Nursing
Service Reserve and gave it her name. When the South African
War broke out a very high proportion of the nurses who went
to it were those of Princess Christian's Army Nursing Service
Reserve. Indeed, the Central British Red Cross* Committee
agreed, a month before hostilities broke out, that, 'all offers of
assistance from nursing sisters should be referred to the Army
Nursing Service Reserve'.

At the outbreak of the war there was one Lady Superintendent
of the Army Nursing Service. Her name was Miss Norman. Miss
Caulfeild, the Lady Superintendent at the Herbert Hospital, had
retired in 1894, and the post of Lady Superintendent at Woolwich
was abolished. Mrs Deeble, the Lady Superintendent at Netley,
had retired in 1889 and her place was taken by Miss Norman.

The Lady Superintendent had nineteen Superintendent Nurses
under her when the war started and the Army Nursing Service
was quite small. But, thanks to the Reserves, about 1,400 women
nurses finally went to South Africa. By the time the war was
over there were twenty-two general hospitals in South Africa,
each with over five hundred beds.

The Boer War was, after the American Civil War, the first
major conflict to be fought with modern weapons. It was also
the first time since Agincourt that Britain fought overseas with an
army consisting solely of Britons. The force which went to South
Africa was the largest Britain had ever sent abroad. The casu-

* The Red Cross movement was founded by Henri Dunant, a Swiss, in
1864. The emblem of the Red Cross is the Swiss flag in reverse. The
British Red Cross Society grew out of the National Society for Aid to
the Sick and Wounded in War.

alties were proportionately high, particularly in the early stages, and the nurses were desperately needed.

Princess Christian's nurses' original strength was only a hundred, but their numbers increased rapidly. They were controlled, before the war broke out, by a specially constituted Committee under Princess Christian's Presidency, but during the war control passed to the War Department. The nurses in the Reserve were paid during the hostilities; before, their services had been voluntary. The Princess's personal interest in her nurses remained intense.

The Medical Department of the Army had been reorganized shortly before the outbreak of the South African War. The RAMC came into being on 23 June, 1898. It was thus only a year old when it was called upon to tend the sick and wounded of the huge army needed to subdue the Boers.

The difficulties with which the RAMC and the Army Nursing Service had to contend were immense, and not the least of them was transport. The British Army was spread over much of South Africa, and where the army was, the casualties were. Many injuries were caused by the expert marksmanship of the Boer farmers but the greatest number of patients suffered from disease. Princess Christian herself lost her son, Prince Christian Victor, through enteric, an affliction that killed eight thousand other soldiers. Figures of casualties in war are always horrifyingly large and one of the many tragedies of the South African War was that the high casualty figures were due to sickness. The battles which the RAMC and the Sisters had to fight were for hygiene and sanitation.

Princess Christian's Reserve nurses were not the only ones to swell the numbers of the Army Nursing Service during the South African War. The Princess of Wales had already shown sympathy for the work and welfare of nurses and she organized the dispatch of Sisters to the war from the London Hospital, in which she took a particular interest. She referred to 'my military nurses' at that time, little knowing that it would not be long before military nurses were to become a service established by Royal Warrant and that the name the service would bear would be her own.

Eighty nurses also went to South Africa from Canada, Australia and New Zealand. There is an illuminating passage in *Three Centuries of Canadian Nursing*, by John Murray Gibbon in collaboration with Mary S. Mathewson (Macmillan, Canada, 1947) which reads:

'An order was issued that Canadian nurses in South Africa were to be granted the rank, pay and allowance of Lieutenant in the Army. Another quite important item to those Nursing Sisters was the costume, which was khaki in colour and consisted of a short bicycle skirt, a Russian blouse with shoulder straps and service buttons, brown leather belt and boots, khaki sailor hat with a little red brush, white collar and cuffs, apron with bib and, as an afterthought, an English Army Nursing Service Cap.'

The uniform sounds more comfortable and practical than the long skirts worn by the Sisters from Britain who, unlike the Canadian Sisters, were not granted military rank, although they were considered to be of officer status.

The skirts worn by the Army Nursing Service and the Reserve were only a little shorter than those worn by their colleagues at home, reaching down to just above the ankle. In the hot weather and during the rainy season they must have been impractical indeed, especially when living and nursing in tents. The Sisters in South Africa wore, with their grey dresses, white head veils, aprons and cuffs while nursing and serge dresses, also grey, with straw boaters with a scarlet ribbon round the crown when off duty. A black leather pouch holding forceps, a pair of scissors and a probe was suspended from a silver-buckled belt. They also carried white parasols lined with scarlet, which were elegant and intended to be practical in the African sun.

The first four Canadian Sisters went to South Africa with the First Contingent of the Canadian Army in November 1899 (a month after the outbreak of hostilities). The following January four additional nursing Sisters were chosen (there were a hundred and ninety volunteers). In 1901 the Canadian Nursing Service was organized as an integral part of the Army Medical Corps and six of the original eight nurses of the First and Second Contingents formed its nucleus and four of them did a second tour of duty in South Africa from November 1901 until July 1902.

One of them, Georgina Fane Pope, wrote in her report after her first tour of duty with the First Contingent, of which she was Superintendent:

'We remained at Wynberg for nearly a month when No 3 General Hospital of 600 beds was pitched under canvas at Rondebosch, a few miles away . . . and we with three English Army Sisters (one of them was Superintendent) formed the nursing staff there. Here we arrived on Christmas Day (1899) and remained almost six months, having at times very active service, sometimes covered with sand during a "Cape south-easter", at others deluged with a forerunner of the coming rainy season, and at all times in terror of scorpions and snakes as bedfellows.'

Miss Pope's report was a long one. She wrote of being sent to Kroonstadt as Acting Superintendent at four hours notice with another Canadian Sister and 'eight English Reserve Sisters'. After 'most uncomfortable travelling' the group arrived, having been reinforced by five Sisters from New South Wales. The pattern of co-operation with the Commonwealth nursing services which exists today had been set.

As regards the sick and wounded, Miss Pope had this to say: 'We found "Tommy Atkins" a very good patient and a fine fellow, always grateful, generally cheerful, bearing loss of limb, loss of health and many minor discomforts with a fortitude that satisfied our best ideas of British pluck, while his consideration for the presence of "the Sister" was at times quite touching.' She was not alone in this opinion.

Perhaps the final sentence of her report can be said to express the opinion Tommy Atkins had of the Sisters who looked after him:

'I cannot close this report without saying that it has been to me and my Sisters a great privilege to serve the Empire in assisting the sick and wounded in faraway South Africa, and if we have lessened their sufferings as we endeavoured to do, we are amply repaid for the hardships which are necessarily encountered in such a campaign.'

The British lost twenty-two thousand men during the South African War. Two-thirds of that number died of disease. Compared with the casualties of the First World War perhaps they may be considered slight, but that was to be a very different kind of war.

It would seem that in South Africa most conditions 'entailing a fever' were classified as enteric fever. One English Sister in the Reserve caught such a fever during an epidemic and recalled that the diet prescribed consisted of chicken soup and cornflour pudding and 'small amounts of milk donated by a Boer farmer'. The soup and the pudding never found favour with her afterwards.

The Sisters went nearer the front line (if the fluid nature of the South African campaign merits the use of such a term) than they had done hitherto, and to live under canvas was by no means the exception.

There were three types of hospital in South Africa, Field, Stationary and General Base. Officially the Sisters did not work in the Field Hospitals, but on occasion Sisters were to be found in these poorly equipped mobile hospitals which moved with the army. A central marquee, which was both dressing station and operating theatre, formed the heart of a Field Hospital; the bell tents surrounding it could hold approximately a hundred patients. The so-called Stationary Hospitals were also mobile. They too were small but better equipped and officially had four Sisters attached to each. The General Base Hospitals where the casualties were finally taken, were large, and generally in or near the ports. These had a minimum staff of twenty nurses.

The nurses worked in hospital trains for the first time during the South African War, looking after the patients on their way to the Base Hospitals, after they had been discharged from the 'Stationary' Hospitals.

The ambulances in those days were primitive indeed: wagons drawn by mules and driven by Kaffirs. A volunteer ambulance corps had been raised early in the campaign. These untrained stretcher bearers were a mixed crowd of men: refugees from the Transvaal and men who had lost their jobs because of the war;

7. *Queen Alexandra, President of the Service which bore her name.*

8. *The original design of the badge. '. . . it was approved by the King and registered as the ensignia of the QAIMNS in 1905. The Queen chose the cross of the Order of Dannebrog from her native Denmark to form the basis of the badge.'*

9. *A medical ward in the Station Hospital, Poona, in 1904.*

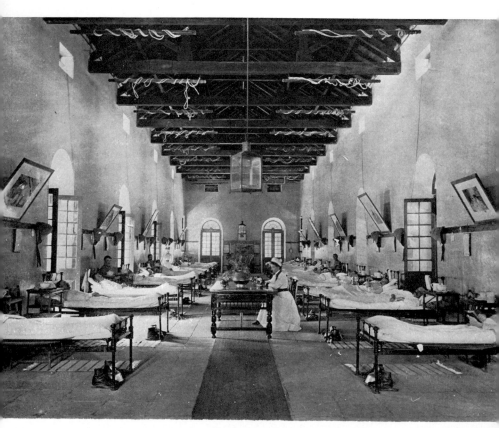

shop assistants, lawyers and miners, they were known as 'body-snatchers'. But Tommy Atkins soon, and with cause, dignified this title to 'pick-me-ups' and 'catch-'em-alive-oh's'.

Sir Frederick Treves wrote of these bearers in *The Tales of a Field Hospital*: 'They entered the camp a thriftless crowd, and came out of it a company of handy men.' He also wrote, after the Battle of Colenso in December 1899, that at Chieveley, whither Buller's army retreated following his unsuccessful attempt to relieve Ladysmith, there was only one house, the station master's. Treves said:

'It had been effectually looted after the Boer fashion, but it would have done well as a resting-place for the four nurses who came up with the hospital. The house, however, had been taken possession of and the nurses had to contemplate either a night in the open or in the waiting-room of the station. As this latter room had been used as a stable by the Boers, it was not in much request. It served, however, as a place for the depositing of personal baggage and for the preparing of such food as it was possible to prepare – chiefly, indeed, for the making of tea. The question of where to sleep was soon solved by the necessities of the position. These ill-housed women, as a matter of fact, were hard at work all Friday, all Saturday, and all Saturday night. They seemed oblivious to fatigue, to hunger, or to any need for sleep. Considering that the heat was intense, that the thirst which attended it was distressing and incessant, that water was scarce, and that the work in hand was heavy and trying, it was wonderful that they came out of it so little the worse in the end. Their ministrations to the wounded were invaluable and beyond all praise. They did a service during those distressful days which none but nurses could have rendered, and they set to all at Chieveley an example of unselfishness, self-sacrifice and indefatigable devotion to duty. They brought to many of the wounded and the dying that comfort which men are little able to evolve, or are uncouth in bestowing, and which belongs especially to the tender, undefined and undefinable ministrations of women.'

These four nurses were in fact serving in a Field Hospital, commanded by Treves, and that passage in his book is a vignette

D

of the work the nurses did during the South African War and of the standard of behaviour of the military nurses of the time.

There were nurses in Ladysmith during the seige and of these Owen S. Watkins wrote in *Chaplains at the Front*:

'Of the Nursing Sisters I cannot write as I should like: for no words could describe all that they did and all that they endured. It was a marvel of heroic endurance for gentle women to live in a camp exposed to wind and rain, heat and cold, almost perpetual duty, each with some sixty patients under her care, and most of them in a dying condition; whilst their food was unpalatable and barely sufficient to satisfy the craving of hunger . . . For in their noble devotion, cheerfully they sacrificed years out of their lives in order that they might add to the comfort of "Tommy". To my certain knowledge, the Sisters continued at their duty with the temperature at 103°, and with their own hands tried to concoct dainty dishes out of the small material at their command in order to tempt their patients' appetites, whilst they themselves were faint and dizzy from lack of the food which their weariness caused them to turn from with nausea. Truly, without exception, they were heroines deserving of the Royal Red Cross.'

The Royal Red Cross to which Watkins referred had been instituted by Queen Victoria on St George's Day, 1883. The Royal Warrant stated that the Decoration was to be conferred 'upon any ladies, whether subjects or foreign persons, who may be recommended by Our Secretary of State for War for special exertions in providing for the nursing of sick and wounded soldiers and sailors of Our Army and Navy'. In George V's reign the words 'or Our Air Force in the field' were added.

The Decoration is awarded in two classes: recipients of the 1st Class are known as Members and those of the 2nd Class, Associates. Associates may be promoted to be Members and further recognitions of 'special exertions' are awarded by an addition of a Bar. The 2nd Class of the Order and the Bar were instituted in 1931. The Order itself is made of gold and red enamel and the lowest of the four limbs carries the date 1883. The other three bear the words 'Faith', 'Hope' and 'Charity'. In the centre there is a medallion of Queen Victoria's veiled and diademed head.

It is scarcely surprising that Miss Nightingale and Mrs Deeble were among the first recipients of the Decoration. Sister Sarah Anne Terrot, alone of the Sellonites who had served in the Crimea, also received it, and Miss Loch, in India, was similarly decorated in 1891. She suspected that two of the Nursing Sisters who went on field service in 1888 might get it when she was asked to recommend which of the Sisters she considered deserved special consideration, and, typically of her and in the fashion of her time, she wrote, 'Wouldn't it be jolly?'

They did get it and so did she.

While the war was still in progress a Royal Commission was appointed, Queen Victoria signing the order for it at Osborne on 24 July, 1900, to report on the 'Care and Treatment of the Sick and Wounded during the South African Campaign'. The six Commissioners went to South Africa and presented their Report in January 1901, the month in which Queen Victoria died.

A part of it reads:

'The nurses employed in this war have shown great devotion, and many have lost their lives in the discharge of their duties. Scarcely any complaints have been made during this campaign with regard to the nurses. The soldiers have much appreciated their service, and seem to prefer to be attended by them to being attended to by orderlies. But, bearing in mind the ordinary conditions of a military hospital, we think that it will always be necessary, even in fixed hospitals and in suitable wards, that the employment of nurses should be supplemented by that of properly trained orderlies.'

The use of the words 'suitable wards' is clarified earlier in the Report in a passage which said: 'Venereal cases clearly ought to be treated only by orderlies'. It goes on to say: 'In cases of this kind nurses are unsuitable, but for enteric and other fever patients . . . would appear to be far better than orderlies, and their general employment in fixed hospitals ought to be now generally recognized by the authorities, and be provided for in future wars.'

The Report states that transport in South Africa consisted of trains, often open trucks, wagons and stretchers, and among the 'Suggestions with a view of remedying defects' was 'The improvement of the existing ambulance wagons'. The section relating to nurses in the 'Suggestions' reads: 'The employment, to a greater extent than that recognized and practised until the later stages of this war, of nurses in fixed hospitals for the care of the wounded and of fever and dysenteric patients, and such others as can properly be nursed by females [should be implemented].' It was recommended that there should be trained officers for sanitary duties and 'regulations and provisions which will enable surgeons and trained orderlies in sufficient numbers to be rapidly obtained and added to the ordinary staff of the RAMC in the event of a great war: and that will also ensure a rapid supply of all hospital and other equipment required for the due care of the sick and wounded in such a war.'

The use of the words 'great war' was prophetic. When that time came the recommendations of the Royal Commission had been put into effect.

CHAPTER 6

Queen Alexandra's Imperial Military Nursing Service

THE Treaty of Vereeniging which finally ended the South African War was not signed until 31 May, 1902, but action was already being taken to put the recommendations of the Report of the Royal Commission on the 'Care and Treatment of the Sick and Wounded during the South African Campaign' into effect.

In the same year as the presentation of the Report a Committee was set up to recommend a scheme for the reorganization of the Army Medical and Nursing Services. St John Brodrick, the Secretary of State for War, was in the Chair and Sir Frederick Treves, who had written so warmly of the nurses in South Africa, was one of the members of the Committee.

The Committee sat for several days, starting on 5 July, 1901. The first few meetings were devoted to the RAMC. On 22 July, at the fifth meeting, the discussion turned to nursing and there was argument as to whether or not the Army Nursing Service should be amalgamated with the Indian Nursing Service. It was stated by Surgeon-General Hooper that there were at that time thirty-nine nurses, nine nursing Sisters and four Superintendents in India. He also revealed that the nurses were recruited from a register kept of 'social and professional qualifications'. Preference was given, when possible, to relatives of military officers and it was clear that Surgeon-General Hooper wanted the recruiting system kept that way. At this meeting the duties of the Matron-in-Chief of the new Service were also discussed, as was the title, Principal Matron, a term which had not hitherto been used. The Committee enthusiastically agreed that the new Queen should be asked to assume the Presidency of the new Service, which would be an amalgamation of the existing Army Nursing Service and the Indian Nursing Service. It was agreed it should be known as Queen Alexandra's Imperial Military Nursing Service.

In the event the Indian Nursing Service became Queen Alexandra's Military Nursing Service for India, with Miss Loch its first Senior Lady Superintendent, and the Royal Warrant bringing the QAIMNS into being a year later referred to it as being comprised of 'Our Army Nursing Service' only.

Queen Alexandra was, of course, perfectly well aware that she would be asked to be President of the new Service, as she was aware that it would carry her name. In February 1901, only a month after Edward VII's accession, the Chairman of the London Hospital, the Hon Sydney Holland, had prepared a memorandum for her at her request, which she then permitted to be circulated.

The memorandum dealt with many aspects of military nursing. Sydney Holland suggested, for instance, that promotion should be by merit and not seniority, saying: 'To have an incompetent Sister placed over more capable women is fatal to discipline and disastrous to good nursing.' He suggested that a badge should be given to every nurse in the Service and that these badges should be 'a mark of merit, and not a mere advertisement of good intentions'. These two small quotes from the long memorandum give some idea as to how it was hoped the Service would evolve.

And so, by Royal Warrant, signed on 27 March, 1902, Queen Alexandra's Imperial Military Nursing Service came into being.

The Warrant was signed by Edward VII and countersigned by St John Brodrick. It read:

'Whereas We deem it expedient to further provide for the nursing services of Our Army: Our Will and Pleasure is that an Imperial Military Nursing Service, to be designated the Queen Alexandra's Imperial Military Nursing Service and comprising Our Army Nursing Service, shall be established and the regulations contained in the Warrant of Our late Royal Mother, dated 26 October, 1900, shall be amended as follows . . .'

The regulations referred to concerned pay and pensions in the army generally. The Warrant covered Nursing Sisters, who received thirty pounds a year for their first year of service, with increments of two pounds a year until the limit of fifty pounds was reached. Under the new Warrant, Sisters were to receive thirty-seven pounds and ten shillings at the beginning of their service.

Queen Alexandra's Imperial Military Nursing Service was a noble sounding name, and that is how Sydney Holland had hoped it would be. He had written in his Memorandum: 'There are regiments called "Queen's Own" and "King's Own" and in the case of barristers known as the "Devil's Own". Nurses might therefore belong to a Corps called "Queen Alexandra's Own" and the name would give great gratification and honour to those serving in it.' The use of the Queen Consort's name had the result Sydney Holland intended and Queen Alexandra, who took the greatest personal interest in the Service, undoubtedly considered it to be her 'own'.

The first meeting of the Nursing Board was held on 21 April, 1902. Surgeon-General Taylor, Director-General Army Medical Services was in the Chair. Countess Roberts, the Vice-President, was there, so too were Sir Frederick Treves, Surgeon-General Keogh, Sidney Jane Browne, the first Matron-in-Chief, QAIMNS, the Matrons of St Thomas's and King's College Hospitals, Viscountess Downe and Sydney Holland. It was decided that there should be fortnightly meetings and that the Board should consist of three matrons of hospitals with medical schools, an India Office representative, two of Her Majesty's nominees (to serve for a period of three years) and 'two members of the Advisory Board, AMS, one of whom shall be a civilian'. These members, of course, were in addition to the Queen as President, the Vice-President and the DGAMS (or an officer nominated by him).

Surgeon-General Taylor said at this meeting: 'It has now been recognized that a further extension of the female nursing system in peace is necessary, and that the utility of female nurses in war is capable of an extension hitherto not contemplated.' He concluded with the words which many QAs claim describe not only the essence of their chosen profession or calling, but which actually brought it into existence at that first meeting of the Nursing Board: 'We believe that an extension of powers of the Matron, of the Sisters and of the nurses in military hospitals will be of enormous advantage to the officer in charge of the hospital, through him to the General Officer Commanding, and ultimately to the Army at large.'

The fortnightly meetings of the Nursing Board were held in the Commander-in-Chief's Levée Room, Horseguards, Whitehall. Queen Alexandra attended the second meeting. She said she would give a badge to the new Service (following Sydney Holland's suggestion of the previous year), and this she did.

It took some while for her to design the badge and for it to be made and it was more than two years before it was approved by the King and registered as the ensignia of the QAIMNS in 1905. The Queen chose the cross of the Order of Dannebrog from her native Denmark to form the basis of the badge. It is a Maltese cross and it forms the centre of the Order. 'Dannebrog' means Cloth of the Danes and its origin dates back to the traditional date of 15 June, 1219. King Waldemar the Victorious of Denmark was on a crusade in Estonia. A piece of cloth is said to have fluttered down from the sky and a voice was heard to say, 'Under this sign you will be victorious'. King Waldemar's retainers picked up the cloth, or flag. It was red with a white cross on it extending to the edges of the material. The campaign was indeed a victorious one. The episode reputedly happened near Reval or Tallinn, and the Danish Royal Standard was first flown at the Seige of Reval or Tallinn. Tallinn, capital of Estonia, is an Estonian word: Reval means City of the Danes. The coat of arms of Tallinn consisted of a white cross on a red ground, so it is not unlikely that such a flag was in use during that period of King Waldemar's reign.

The motto of the Order of Dannebrog, *Sub Cruce Candida*, derives from this story. It was appropriate for Queen Alexandra to choose it as the motto for her Service and it was formally adopted at the thirtieth meeting of the Nursing Board in 1903.

The Dannebrog also formed part of the badges of the 19th Royal Hussars and the Green Howards, but the QA's badge remains as it was designed and registered. It is worn today, as it was then, on the right side of a scarlet cape over a dress of grey. Only the name of the Service on the badge has been changed. Now it reads: Queen Alexandra's Royal Army Nursing Corps.

CHAPTER 7

The First Years

I N those early days at the beginning of the century the Nursing
Board discussed every detail pertaining to the new Service.
The uniform was approved. The grey dresses and scarlet capes,
muslin caps and grey outdoor bonnets were all reviewed as were,
of course, salaries, pensions and conditions of service. Netley was
not to be the training school for military nurses any longer and
candidates had to have had at least three years training in a
civil hospital behind them. The hospitals whose training the
Nursing Board recognized were listed.

The candidates were carefully chosen, much attention being
given both to their character, education and social standing as
well as to their training and experience.

In the summer of 1902 the Nursing Board recommended that
Sisters of Princess Christian's Army Nursing Service Reserve who
had served with the army in the field in South Africa should
be allowed to count such service towards their pension if
selected for the QAIMNS.

The discipline and duties of Matrons and Sisters were thrashed
out at the fortnightly meetings. The Matrons' duties ranged from
assisting at all operations through keeping accounts to fixing
hours for Sisters and staff nurses and dealing with their confi-
dential reports.

There was a humanity in the running of the QAIMNS from
its earliest beginnings, as well as strict discipline. The Nursing
Board recommended that Sisters be requested to learn about the
home circumstances of men invalided out of the army, that they
should tell Matron about them and that she in turn should tell
the Officer-in-Charge of the hospital. Sisters were also forbidden
to accept presents of 'any kind from any patient, or friend of any
patient, whether during his illness or after his death, recovery or
departure'.

In October, 1902, the Nursing Board considered and rejected a proposal from Queen Alexandra's sister-in-law, Princess Christian, President of the Army Nursing Service Reserve Committee, that the Nursing Board be represented on her Committee by the Matron-in-Chief and one nursing member of the Board. As the war in South Africa was over it was felt that there was no further need for Reserve nurses: the QAIMNS had no intention that year of interfering with Princess Christian's Reserve.

In the same month the Nursing Board's requirements for nurses were for twenty-seven hospitals excluding those in South Africa, the hospitals being in the United Kingdom as well as such parts of the Empire as Canada, Gibraltar and Jamaica. At that time the total required strength of the QAIMNS was, apart from the Matron-in-Chief, who worked at the War Office and two Principal Matrons (one in South Africa and one acting as Assistant to the Matron-in-Chief), twenty-seven Matrons, fifty Sisters and a hundred and fifty staff nurses. But more QAs were needed in South Africa, where much of the army was still stationed, as well as in those military hospitals with less than a hundred beds.

In December, the Nursing Board decided that promotions should be by merit and not seniority (Sydney Holland's wisdom was well heeded) and the first entrants to the QAIMNS, as opposed to those who had originally belonged to the Army Nursing Service, were approved. Among these was Miss E. H. Becher of the Army Nursing Service Reserve. She was admitted as Principal Matron and worked with the Matron-in-Chief in London. Miss S. J. Browne, the original Matron-in-Chief, (she became Dame Sidney Browne) remained in that office until 1906 and was succeeded by Miss C. H. Keer, who had been accepted by the Nursing Board to be Principal Matron in South Africa in January 1903. Miss Keer had previously been in the Army Nursing Service. She remained as Matron-in-Chief until 1910 when she was succeeded by Miss (later Dame Ethel) Becher.

In February 1903, more Matrons, Sisters and staff nurses were accepted by the Nursing Board. Many were rejected and the reasons given by the Board included the candidates having an 'unsuitable appearance', being over age (they had to be between twenty-five and thirty-five) and several who were considered to be of 'unsatisfactory social status'. Some had poor reports from their Matrons.

The Nursing Board had set the pattern for QAs to be regarded as members of an exclusive service and by the time the First World War broke out the QAs were rightly considered to be the *élite* among the thousands of nurses who served in the war.

Among the Matrons to be accepted in February 1903, was Miss E. M. McCarthy. She had served with the Army Nursing Service Reserve in South Africa from December 1899, until July 1902, and previously had been at the London Hospital for eight years. She, too, was to become a Matron-in-Chief.

The QAIMNS consolidated its position of being allied to, but not actually part of, the army under the firm but benevolent guidance of its President and the Nursing Board during the years leading up to the First World War. The Director-General of the Army Medical Services was, of course, on the Nursing Board and the Matron-in-Chief was responsible for the running of the Service with his concurrence. The Matrons by now had full charge of the hospital wards as well as of the syllabus of instruction used in preparing RAMC orderlies for their nursing certificates. The link between the RAMC and the QAIMNS became an increasingly close one as the years went on. The days of untrained soldier orderlies such as described by Miss Loch in 1890 were truly over.

The RAMC moved the Army Medical School from Netley to temporary premises in London in 1902. The School became the Royal Army Medical College and in 1907 moved into its new building on the Thames, next door to the Tate Gallery on Millbank. Very close to the College a new military hospital was built. It was constructed on the now familiar 'Nightingale' pattern, and was named after Queen Alexandra. She and Edward VII opened it in July 1905.

Two years later the Bowen Road Military Hospital was opened in Hong Kong, and it is recorded that sedan chairs were chartered there 'to carry the sick from the lower levels up the hill each morning'. In spite of the experience gained in South Africa, it

still seemed quite adventurous in those days for QAs to serve
as far away from home as Hong Kong. But the principle had
now been accepted that QAs should serve all over the world
wherever the British Army was stationed.

As sanitary and preventative methods improved, so did the
health of the army. In Malta, where military nurses had long
since served, the fever known as 'Malta Fever' had ceased to be
a regular hazard since the fever baccillus had been discovered in
goats' milk and the troops were prohibited from buying it. It was
no longer necessary to have as many hospitals in Malta, and in
India, Egypt and the west coast of Africa, malaria and enteric
were becoming less prevalent among the soldiers, partly because
of improvement in sanitary conditions and partly because the
age of inoculation and the recognition of the dangers of the
mosquito had arrived.

At Netley in 1907 two Sisters (one of them was to become
Dame Ann Beadsmore Smith and succeed Dame Ethel Becher
as Matron-in-Chief in 1919) nursed a certain Dr Kunze who was
Staff Surgeon attached to the German Emperor's yacht, *Hohen-
zollern*. He had a bad attack of pleurisy and in January 1908,
the Emperor presented brooches to the Sisters in recognition of
their skilful nursing. Edward VII gave the Sisters permission to
wear the brooches given to them by his cousin.

That year was a particularly difficult one for the Nursing
Board. The Territorial Army had come into being and with it
the Territorial Force Nursing Service, later to become the
Territorial Army Nursing Service. The time had come for the
QAIMNS to have a Reserve. Princess Christian's Army Nursing
Service Reserve became the QAIMNS (R) and the Queen was,
of course, its President in the same way as she was President of
the Advisory Council of the Territorial Force Nursing Service.

Princess Christian had always chosen the nurses for her Army
Nursing Service Reserve personally, and she doubtless had feel-
ings of regret that her name was no longer to be associated with
the Reserve. From a letter she wrote to St John Brodrick it is
clear that she was deeply disappointed that she neither had a
seat on the Nursing Board in her capacity of President of the

Army Nursing Service Reserve nor, later, that her request for two members of the Board to sit on her Committee had been turned down. She signed the letter Helena, her baptismal name. She was known in the family as Lenchen, but it is by her husband's name that she is remembered for her services to military nursing (and indeed to civil nursing and hospitals). She died in 1923.

On 28 December, 1908, there was an earth tremor in Malta, followed by a tidal wave. News by wireless swiftly followed that the Sicilian coastal town of Messina had been destroyed by earthquake. At the request of the King of Italy, the Royal Navy transported a relief party of RAMC personnel to Messina two days later. A Field Ambulance section went, taking with them a Stationary Hospital with stores and rations for ten days. Some of the wounded were taken on board HMS *Duncan* and HMS *Minerva* and tended in the dressing stations. The hospital was set up in what had been the market place in nearby Catona. Catona, across the narrow Straits of Messina, had also been devastated by the earthquake, and it was there that two Sisters of the QAIMNS, with two volunteer nurses, also from Malta, were sent when they disembarked from *Duncan* during the morning of 2 January, 1909. The four women were allotted tents near the Officers' Mess tent and the Stewards' Store tent. And there they nursed until 15 January, when the whole party returned to Malta.

QAs had experienced a disaster in peacetime and had brought nursing skill and comfort to the victims. It was not to be their last such experience.

Edward VII and Florence Nightingale both died in the following year. A new era had begun.

CHAPTER 8

The First World War

D AME ETHEL BECHER became Matron-in-Chief in 1910.
The two previous holders of this office had retired after
four years. But after 1914 everything changed and the
Matron-in-Chief remained at the War Office until 1919.

Dame Sidney Browne had become Matron-in-Chief of the
TFNS at its inception in 1908. She had also been the first Matron-
in-Chief, QAIMNS and was destined to become the first President
of the Royal College of Nursing in 1922. She remained in
charge of the TFNS until the war was over. Her Territorial
nurses, with those of the QAIMNS (R) quickly swelled the ranks
of nurses in Territorial and civil hospitals and nursing and
convalescent homes (quite apart from the regular military hospitals) where army patients were cared for, as did members
of the British Red Cross and the Order of St John of Jerusalem.

There were just under three hundred nurses in the QAIMNS
in August 1914. By the end of the year the numbers had risen,
through the Reserve, to 2,223 and when the war ended 10,404
trained nurses had enrolled.

Lists of figures can be meaningless, but of the Reserve in 1914,
two hundred were ready to be called up at twenty-four hours
notice and a further six hundred were available.

There were also nearly 9,000 trained and partially trained
nurses, who were members of the Voluntary Aid Detachments,
who served in military hospitals during the war. Many of them
did the work of orderlies; all were of great value. They served
under and with the QAIMNS.

This great company of women all came under the jurisdiction of
Dame Ethel Becher and if she was regarded as a formidable
lady, as indeed she was, then her task was also formidable in
the extreme.

The trepidation with which the Matron-in-Chief was regarded

is evidenced by a little known episode concerning a memorial to Florence Nightingale. The QAIMNS had subscribed towards a memorial window for the chapel at Millbank which had been donated privately and anonymously. Through a series of mis-understandings the design of the window was not approved by the authorities responsible for the furnishing of the chapel. After considerable discussion and argument the original window was removed and a different window put in its place. (The present window, depicting the three women finding the empty tomb and the Ascension, has been at Millbank for sixty years. It is earmarked for the chapel in the new, as yet unfinished, hospital in Woolwich which will replace the Queen Alexandra Hospital, Millbank when it is pulled down in order to extend the Tate Gallery.)

In December 1914 Miss Becher received a letter telling her that the original window had been sent to a firm in Scotland where it would be stored and re-erected wherever she wished without charge to the QAs. The letter shows that every effort was made to spare the Matron-in-Chief any personal embarrass-ment about what had clearly been a most distressing matter for those in charge of the chapel furnishings. The writer of the letter, an officer in the RAMC, said that it had been planned for the substitution to be postponed until after her retirement in April 1914. Evidently it had then become known that her appointment had been extended until September of that year. The war broke out on 4 August and when Miss Becher's appoint-ment was further extended she had to be told of the reasons behind the substitution of the Florence Nightingale window while still Matron-in-Chief. This is something which the writer of the letter had hoped to avoid. The Matron-in-Chief cannot have enjoyed being informed that she had exceeded her authority as regards the QAs' memorial to Florence Nightingale.

When war broke out members of the QAIMNS were wearing their familiar short scarlet capes on duty, with its stiff Alexandra rose at the back between the shoulder blades. (It was said, apocryphally, that the rose was there to prevent Sisters falling asleep on night duty. Equally apocryphally it was said that the cape had been designed to keep the Sisters warm and the officers cool.) The members of the Reserve wore a short grey cape. It did, however, have a scarlet border and a scarlet rose at the back. Their badge had been registered in 1910 and, like the Regulars, they wore it on the right of their capes. The cape of the TFNS also had a scarlet border but the cape was of a bluer grey, and they had their own badge.

The QAs wore ground-length grey dresses and white aprons with square bibs. Off duty they wore thicker capes under long cloaks, always with a grey bonnet tied with a big bow under the chin. The uniform came from Shoolbreds in Tottenham Court Road;* thus equipped they went to war.

In 1915 the bonnets were withdrawn and replaced by grey felt hats; grey coats were worn instead of the long cloaks. Dame Maud McCarthy was responsible for the bonnet being abandoned. Doubtless the substitution of the long cloak by a coat was at her instigation too, for she is remembered as wearing a grey coat in France lined with scarlet satin.

After the Battle of Mons in August 1914, several of the Sisters were sent to the Brittany coast where the sea air and sunshine combined to discolour and bedraggle their bonnets. Dame Maud, who was at Le Mans, sent for her Personal Assistant. She looked at the young woman's bonnet and asked if she had another. On learning that she only had one (The list of uniform requirements specified only one.) she instructed her P.A. to throw it in the wastepaperbasket at once, 'and I will buy you a hat,' she said. She did buy her a hat, and after considerable correspondence with the War Office, hats became part of the uniform of the QAs a year later.

At the War Office Dame Ethel Becher was responsible to the DGAMS for the recruiting, administration and drafting of the entire nursing service under her throughout the war. In each theatre of operations there was a Principal Matron, who was responsible to her. The single exception was Dame Maud McCarthy, Matron-in-Chief to the British Expeditionary Force

---

* Shoolbreds continued to supply the uniforms until they went into liquidation in 1931, when Harrods took over.

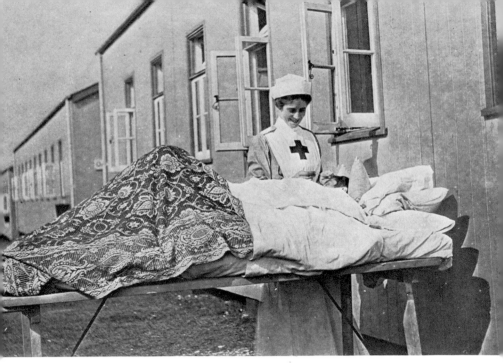

10. *A VAD with a patient at Netley, 1914.*

11. *Members of the QAIMNS (R) on active service during the First World War. 'Camping holidays were rare indeed in pre-1914 England and the QAs learned of the doubtful pleasures of sleeping under canvas in climatic and geographical conditions during the war which were, to say the least, exceedingly irksome.'*

12. *QAs visit the Pyramids while stationed in Egypt during the First World War.*

13. *Dame Maud McCarthy saying good-bye to Sir Douglas Haig on his departure from France, at Boulogne, at the end of the First World War. Miss Barbier is on his right, facing the camera.*

in France and Flanders, who was responsible to GHQ. She was the only head of department to remain with the BEF throughout the war. This is the only instance in the history of the QAs when there have been two Matrons-in-Chief.

The first General Hospital to the BEF landed in France on 12 August. Dame Maud was among the first QAs to cross the Channel.

She was an able administrator and before she left England, within a few days of the outbreak of war, she had the foresight to find and take with her a member of the Reserve who was bilingual in English and French. Dame Maud, who had been born and brought up in Australia, knew her own French was insufficient for the task ahead. The nursing Sister she chose was Isobel Barbier (now Sister Mary Jordan, a member of the Order of St Dominic), one of the first Sisters to join the Reserve in 1914. She worked with Dame Maud throughout the war as her Personal Assistant, and stayed on with her at the War Office for three months, sorting and compiling records until she returned to civil nursing in 1919. Both at Abbeville, Headquarters of the Lines of Communication, where Dame Maud had her HQ, and at St Omer (the GHQ first of Gen Sir John French and then of Gen Sir Douglas Haig, when he became the Commander-in-Chief in 1915) Miss Barbier was known as the ADC. She held a unique position in the Service and, with her inborn administrative gift, resourcefulness, linguistic abilities and humour, she was well qualified to hold it. She was to receive both the RRC and the military division of the MBE.

It was a very different war from the one in South Africa, which Dame Maud had experienced. The Medical Services were better trained and there were more of them, but the hazards of war were as new as they were horrible. Gas and air attacks had been unknown in the Boer War, and both the German and the British armies were now partially mechanized. Trench warfare on such a scale had hitherto been unknown. Generals had never before had such huge armies under their command and the wielding of them in Europe presented problems previously undreamed of.

E

The Medical Services in France and Flanders were not so heavily involved with the treatment and prevention of disease as they had been in South Africa. They had to wrestle instead with the speedy treatment (the importance of speed had been recognized) of wounds inflicted by weapons which had not been devised at the time of the Boer War. The age of machine guns, shrapnel, land mines, mortars and bombs had arrived, as well as tanks, flame-throwers and gas.

The effects of the German gas attacks on the Ypres Salient in 1915 were fearsome. The troops had no defence and the doctors and nurses could no nothing to relieve the agonies of the afflicted. Later in the same year the RAMC devised the first gas masks. As these were improved upon, it became compulsory for all troops to carry them until the war was over. Nevertheless, they were awkward and cumbersome and did little to ease the lot of the British Army – or of the QAs, who had to carry them too. At least the latter seldom had to use them.

Trench feet, trench fever and the nervous ailments loosely known as shell shock were further new hazards with which the military medical authorities had to cope and the troops to bear. The first was caused by standing in waterlogged trenches, the second by lice and the last by a variety of causes created by the war – strain, exhaustion and horrifying and unnatural conditions and experiences.

Dame Maud was indefatigable. She visited Field Units, Casuality Clearing Stations, Hospital Trains, Hospital Barges and Stationary and General Hospitals. She was constantly recognized and warmly greeted as she travelled about London after the war on public transport by ex-soldiers who had seen her on these visits. She and Miss Barbier had a military car, driven by a private soldier. On those long travels Dame Maud used to share with him any food or drink she might have. His admiration for, and loyalty to her were great and he was heard on more than one occasion to say to other drivers, many of whom had cause to grumble at their lot: 'My lady never forgets who's in front of her.' Some years after the Armistice Dame Maud's brother came across this driver and asked him if he still had the inscribed

watch his sister had given him. It transpired that it was considered to be too precious to be worn and was kept under a glass
case in his parlour.

Such was the woman who was responsible for the nursing of
the thousands of casualties in the years between 1914 and 1918
in France and Flanders.

QAs, with their colleagues from the other nursing services,
nursed the casualties of the two Battles of the Marne, and the
Battles of Ypres, Passchendaele, Neuve-Chapelle, Festubert,
Loos, Arras, Cambrai, the Somme, Amiens and the Scarpe. Out
of the chaos, the misery and the mud, the Medical Services, of
whom the QAs were such a large part, brought order, comfort
and, where possible, healing. If Dame Ethel Becher at the War
Office can rightly be described as the Commander, Dame Maud
McCarthy, in the midst of it all, was without doubt the Leader.

Field-Marshal Lord Roberts was the popular hero of the
South African War, where his only son had been killed. He was
the husband of the Vice-President of the Nursing Board and it
was he who, in 1902, had insisted that there should be a QAMNS
in India, where he was at that time Commander-in-Chief. In
November 1914, when eighty-two years of age, he went to France
on a tour of inspection and two days after his arrival at St Omer
was taken ill. He died the following evening, on the 14th. Two
'Red Capes' were appointed to nurse him during his last short
illness, and Dame Maud and Miss Barbier both went to see him
in an upstairs room of a house guarded inside and out by
Gurkhas. He wore, as did all sick soldiers, a red bedjacket. It
had been sent from No 13 Stationary Hospital in Wimereux, a
converted hotel, and in the pocket of the jacket was a handker-
chief with a card pinned to it reading 'Good luck from Queen
Mary'. He received this not because he was a Field-Marshal, but
because he was a sick soldier.

On the night of his death, Miss Barbier was sent to Boulogne
to buy wreaths. A Tommy drove her; otherwise she was alone.
No shop was open, for by the time she arrived it was well after
midnight. She found a nursery garden and roused the owner. By
candlelight she chose the flowers to be used in the wreaths to be

given by the Nursing Staff and the Medical Staff at GHQ, quite apart from all the individual wreaths which she had been told to get. It was still dark when she got back to St Omer.

The wreaths were ready in time and accompanied the body back to England in a ship of the Royal Navy. A military band on the quayside at Boulogne played 'Will ye no come back again?' and the lady nurses of the Army as well as those soldiers of the British and Indian Armies who watched mourned that 'Bobs' had gone. Lady Roberts remained Vice-President of the Nursing Board for three years following her husband's death.

QAs also nursed the King in France. In October 1915, his horse suddenly reared and fell on him while he was inspecting his troops. He was taken to GHQ. In her report Dame Maud wrote:

'I visited the Château . . . and afterwards arranged the conversion of part of No 14 Ambulance Train into a bedroom, for the transfer of His Majesty to the Base. He was seen off by Sir John French and many of the Headquarters Staff, the nurses accompanying him . . . I then received instructions to proceed to Boulogne to see that all arrangements were satisfactory on Hospital Ship *Anglia* . . . I saw him safely established in his bunk. He was accompanied on the voyage by Sir Anthony Bowlby and Sir Bertrand Dawson, as well as the two nurses.'

But the Matron-in-Chief's task in France was by no means a question of just caring for Kings and Field-Marshals. Dame Maud's reports are filled, in meticulous detail, with accounts of casualties among her nurses, the numbers of Casualty Clearing Stations and hospitals and the numbers of nurses staffing them. Recreation (of which there was singularly little: QAs were not allowed to go to dances in France), discipline, living conditions and leave rotas were all her responsibility.

Her annual report for 1916 ended:

'Much has been written and said at different times about the relationship between the trained and the untrained, but anyone who has seen them working together during the weeks following the Battle of the Somme would have realized that any feeling there might have been was only of a most superficial character, and that each was only too anxious to help the other, so that they might the better devote themselves to the service of the sick and wounded.'

The VADs had a champion in the Matron-in-Chief of the BEF and she kept the 'exclusiveness' with which the regular QAs were regarded in its proper proportion.

By 1917 Dame Maud had not only dispensed with the bonnet, but had persuaded Dame Ethel to agree that members of the QAIMNS, QAIMNS (R) and TFNS could wear 'tight-fitting grey caps'. Her report stated: 'These caps were only to be worn in camp or on board ship in windy weather'. The regulars had to have the QAIMNS badge embroidered on the corner of their caps.

Hospital Ship *Salta* was torpedoed off Le Havre in April that year and an Acting Matron, one Sister and seven staff nurses were lost. They had had little time in which to wear their new caps.

Dame Maud was taken ill in March, 1917, with appendicitis and was off duty until 10 August. Miss E. H. Hordley undertook her duties until 19 April, when Miss Ann Beadsmore Smith, Principal Matron in Malta, took over as Acting Matron-in-Chief, BEF. She it was who succeeded Dame Ethel Becher at the War Office in 1919. And she was to succeed Dame Maud McCarthy as Matron-in-Chief, TANS, in 1925.

The King and Queen arrived in France in July, 1917. The King visited his Armies and Queen Mary visited hospitals. Dame Maud was in the Sisters' Hospital at Abbeville, and the Queen went and saw her there and, having ascertained from Miss Mary M. Loughron, QAIMNS (R), an Australian who was nursing her, that the Matron-in-Chief was well enough to travel, invited them both to make the journey earlier than had been planned in the destroyer which was to take the Royal party back to England. And so, on 14 July, they boarded the destroyer at Calais where, according to Miss Loughron, 'The King and Queen greeted us like long lost nieces'. They travelled to London in the Royal Train and a Palace car took them to their 'destination'.

Dame Maud had shared the bombing, shelling and general discomforts of the war on the Western Front (of which extreme fatigue was by no means the least) with all the nurses there. Apart from travelling to England with the King and Queen, she also shared with Miss Loughron another unusual experience, which she did not much enjoy. After she had returned to duty she had to give up a little precious time from her office duties and inspections. Her report reads: 'I was requested to proceed to General Headquarters on 16 September in order to sit for a portrait, which is to be included in Mr Frank Salisbury's painting to commemorate the visit of Their Majesties to France, and which is taking the form of a panel to be added to the famous historic panels at the Royal Exchange, London'.

After the Armistice, while Miss Loughron was Matron of the Peace Conference Hospital in Paris, the French Government commissioned M. Eugene Brenand to do her portrait. She sat wearing her indoor uniform and the portrait hangs with others depicting the Allied participants in the war in the Gallery of Portraits of the Allies in Luxembourg, as the representative of the QAs.

Hospitals were bombed and QAs were among the casualties. One regular wrote in her diary at St Omer on 4 October, 1917: 'Buried the fourth Sister who died of her wounds yesterday. The Last Post I always find so harrowing. It always makes me feel I want to howl at a funeral. The two long notes always seem to mean to me "lie still, lie still" '. The same diary reveals that a month earlier Dame Maud had been in an air raid in St Omer when the officers' hospital was hit. Afterwards she found time to send the Sister* 'such a nice message in her letter to Matron'.

Perhaps one of the most revealing descriptions of the conditions with which the QAs had to contend appears in another diary kept by a QA.† In 1918 she was working in a hospital on a plateau above Deauville. 'This was a new area opening up. There were three large hospitals. This area was called the French Blighty . . . It was found that when the wounded were sent home

* Lilian E. A. Robinson.
† Mary Sybil Tyers.

there was a general feeling in England against sending them out again, especially if they had been wounded several times. However, the need for men was so great, particularly for experienced soldiers, that this sentiment was severely discouraged. One of the MOs told me that the Sisters' duty was to devote our time and skill to helping the recovery of the lightly wounded men so they might return, and that the care of the dangerously wounded or sick was not nearly so important; that the Red Cross and all it stood for – hospitals, doctors, nurses – was a hindrance to any army in the field, although an unavoidable one. It was a hard saying to us Sisters, but I knew what he meant, and did not misunderstand him. The situation of the Allies was getting desperate, and every man counted.'

Like the other QA diarist of the previous year she mentioned the 'many funerals, with the pipers playing a lament'. She went on to say: 'The laments had to be stopped after a while. They had such a saddening effect on all.'

The Military Medal had been instituted in March, 1916, to be awarded to Non-Commissioned Officers and men. Not long afterwards it was extended to women on the recommendation of the Commander-in-Chief in the field 'for devotion to duty under fire'. Although the QAs had been recognized officially as being of officer status since 1904, they were not commissioned officers and were thus eligible for the award. To be devoted to duty had always been expected of QAs; to be so under fire came to be expected of them during the First World War.

By 1918 Dame Maud was sending the medal ribbon of the MM to the QAs who had received the award, stapled to one of her official cards with the words 'With Heartiest Congratulations' printed on the card. She signed these herself. The fact that the medal ribbons were issued in this way may have been due to the fact that some of the recipients were reluctant to wear them. 'The soldiers got the MM for bravery; we were only doing what we had to do', was the attitude.

The mutual respect between the British soldier and the QAs cannot have been better exemplified than by the fact that some of the QA recipients of the MM had to be reprimanded for their modesty. Dame Maud tactfully saw to it that the ribbons were put up.

Dame Maud left France from Boulogne on 5 August, 1919. Representatives from the French Government and all the Medical Services came to see her off. The meticulous records, which she had kept since her arrival in France in a big brown exercise book and an alphabetical note book which Miss Barbier had bought in Boulogne on first arriving in France were taken back to England at the same time. They travelled in tea chests, imposingly labelled as being the records of the Matron-in-Chief, British Expeditionary Force and were addressed to AMD 4, The War Office.

At Dover a porter called out: 'Look at all them records. But she ain't got no blooming gramophone!'

CHAPTER 9

The War in the Middle East

THE responsibilities of the Matron-in-Chief at the War Office were world-wide. There were few QAs in Egypt at the outbreak of the First World War, but as a result of the ill-fated Gallipoli campaign in 1915 hundreds of sick and wounded were taken to Egypt and from September onwards regular contingents of nurses were arriving there, from India as well as from the United Kingdom. Towards the end of the war the flood of casualties from the Middle East into Egypt was so great that it was hard to find accommodation for all the nurses who had been sent there, and harder still to nurse the many who, inevitably, became sick themselves through illness and exhaustion. As usual the QAs proved themselves to be adaptable, and many of their sick were nursed in a small school hospital in Alexandria.

During the Gallipoli campaign QAs never actually landed on the peninsula itself, for there was no room on the narrow crowded beaches for hospital tents. Instead they were based on the Island of Lemnos. The wounded were taken to the port of Mudros on the island by hospital ships, on board which were nurses. On occasions it was necessary for there to be twice as many patients on board as the ships were designed to carry. Apart from tending the wounded in overcrowded conditions the QAs worked on board these ships in a sea infested with U-boats.

One member of the Reserve* wrote in her diary of leaving Mudros harbour in

'a small un-fitted cargo boat of the Clan Line for Suvla Bay. She was a registered Hospital Ship and was painted with a large Red Cross on either side. The casualties were brought off on stretchers laid across rowing boats, strings of which were towed out to us from the shore first-aid posts by small motor craft or tugs – anything in fact that was available. They and we were constantly

* Esmé M. Symonds, née Parkinson.

under fire from the shore . . . The only accommodation for the patients were straw mattresses on the cargo decks . . . Lifting from stretcher to mattresses and all the carrying in between soon played havoc with the backs of the young RAMC orderlies, so we Sisters took over . . . a message came down the hatch "The Colonel says the Sisters are not to do stretcher work". We dutifully replied "Very good, Sir," and just carried on. Someone had to do it.'

The winter of 1915 was a particularly hard one on Lemnos – bitterly cold and windy – and living conditions were difficult. By February 1916, the five hospitals there were moved to Egypt and two of them, with the nurses, went on to German East Africa.

The list of places where QAs served in the Middle East and Mediterranean is a long one. There were many in Malta where numbers of casualties from Gallipoli were taken, and, in 1917, they nursed with the Italian Expeditionary Force, both in hospitals and in Casualty Clearing Stations.

After the withdrawal from Gallipoli the British Army went to Salonika and the Medical Services went with them. By 1917 there were over a thousand trained nurses there and in the surrounding country of Macedonia, including those from Canada and Australia. They nursed in tented as well as hutted hospitals (some of the latter had come from Mudros) and had to contend with malaria and dysentery, both for the troops as well as among themselves and, in 1918, with the influenza epidemic which was to spread into Western Europe.

As well as the illnesses of the area the nurses had to learn to live with other indigenous hazards such as wild dogs, hyenas, ants, sand flies, locusts and, of course, mosquitoes. There were tortoises too and at least one QA made a pet of a baby one, tethering it to the ropes of her tent with a thread of cotton.

The Sisters quickly learned that a hammer and nails were of use in Macedonia and they became adept at constructing dressing tables and cupboards from packing cases with which to furnish their tents. Camping holidays were rare indeed in pre-1914 England and the QAs learned of the doubtful pleasures of sleeping under canvas in climatic and geographical conditions during the war which were, to say the least, exceedingly irksome.

QAs did not only tend the troops. In Salonika in 1917 there was a great fire. Rosabelle Osborne, who was Principal Matron with the British Salonika Force and Army of the Black Sea from August 1917 until July 1920 (she was to become Matron-in-Chief for two years in 1928 and to be Matron-in-Chief TANS from 1931 until 1936) wrote that about fifty houses in the Turkish quarters were demolished by the flames within an hour. Allied lorries ferried nearly 100,000 refugees to safety, and in each of the three camps which the British formed for them there was a hospital tent staffed by two Sisters. Again QAs were helping in a civil disaster.

Another future Matron-in-Chief was Florence May Hodgins, who held the post from 1924 until her retirement in 1928. She had served as Matron of a General Hospital in the Gallipoli campaign whence she went to Egypt and from there, with a staff of nurses, she was sent in 1916 to join a Stationary Hospital in Mesopotamia.* Known as 'Mespot' by the troops, it was a particularly disliked, even dreaded, theatre of war. She travelled from Suez to Kuwait, and then, by sea, past Abadan to Basra. This was true desert country – hot and dry. The sea voyage was hazardous; ships had been sunk in the channel near Abadan. From Basra she went by river to Amara in an Irrawaddy paddle steamer (total war involved such geographical incongruities) with a barge lashed to either side. That part of the journey alone took four days.

The heat in Amara was great and when it was a damp heat the QAs had many cases of heat apoplexy to treat, and dysentery and malaria were commonplace.

Transport in Mesopotamia was difficult in the extreme and casualties had long and painful journeys by small steamers, sailing barges, and even mule-drawn wooden carts, to reach hospital. Miss Hodgins described the patients from Kut, which fell to the Turks in April 1916, after a siege of 143 days, as being in a 'most pitiable state'. Kut was re-taken in 1917 and later

* The official name was changed to Iraq in 1921.

that year Miss Hodgins' hospital (No 23 Stationary Hospital) moved to Baghdad, where it was housed in a Turkish Military Hospital which she described as being 'filthy and verminous'.

In Amara No 23 had been on the bank of the Tigris. It was entirely under canvas and had a thousand beds, following a rapid expansion. During the rainy season the Sisters had to wear gum boots all day.

Conditions in Baghdad were very different. The flat-roofed French-style houses of the city were a delight after tents and, as Miss Hodgins said, the Sisters had not seen gardens for 'a long time'.

Other Sisters saw gardens in the country known in those days as Palestine. They also saw, and nursed, a great many wounded as the Turks retreated. After Gen Allenby occupied Jerusalem in 1917 they nursed in the Holy City and saw the Garden of Gethsemene.

In the autumn of 1918, only a month before the Armistice, fourteen QAs went to North Russia. The P & O liner *Kalyan* had been converted into a hospital ship and had seen active service in Egypt and Salonika. In order to sail as far north as Archangel, the only port to which the Allies could try to bring assistance to the remnants of the Russian Imperial Army, *Kalyan* had to undergo extensive alterations to fit her for the cold. Water pipes were encased in asbestos, radiators were installed and the ship's sides were lined with inner wooden walls filled with sawdust. The refitting was done in Cardiff, where the Sisters joined her, and where the Lascars were replaced by a British crew since it was thought that Lascars would not be able to withstand the cold of the Arctic. The voyage took just under a fortnight.

Although the Sisters did not wear trousers (over twenty years were to elapse before QAs went to war in battledress) their clothes were similar to the special kit issued to the men: leather jerkins, windproof sheepskin-lined coats, and caps with fur peaks and ear flaps.

In Archangel *Kalyan* became a hospital, as opposed to a hospital ship. She was moored to a wharf and remained there until her return to the United Kingdom eight months later. The QAs did all their nursing on board. The other hospitals and medical units were staffed, as regards female nursing staff, by ladies of the Russian Red Cross.

The Front was over two hundred miles away and the methods of transport varied; none were comfortable. Until the River Dvina froze the patients were brought to *Kalyan* by barge. Then railway lines were laid on the ice, but patients (who, apart from the British, included Americans, French, Italians and a few Russians) came in fur-lined sleeping bags by horsedrawn open sleighs. Not unnaturally, knowledge of the treatment of frostbite had to be put to use in a practical form. It was not a complaint with which the Sisters had been accustomed to deal.

In May, 1919, icebreakers came, enabling troopships to reach Archangel with reliefs and later that month *Kalyan,* with the rest of the original Force sent to North Russia, sailed for home. The Great War had been over for seven months when *Kalyan* docked in Leith in June, 1919.

The nursing services had been bombed, torpedoed and undergone artillery bombardment. Many of them had never been abroad until they went on active service. They had worked under climatic conditions of every kind and had nursed men mutilated by war and sick with diseases of which, to quote Dame Maud McCarthy, 'the truly awful epidemic of influenza and pneumonia' in 1918 was a part. They had written letters for their patients and to their patients' relatives. They had corresponded, too, with the bereaved, sent photographs of their patients' graves when that was possible and received letters of thanks and, in many cases, the outpourings of broken hearts.

Some of them died. Most of them numbered among the bereaved. They had laughed when they could in public and they had cried in private. They gave comfort to their patients and to one another. Many of them became ill from sheer fatigue. Comparatively few of them ever saw the Garden of Gethsemane; all of them learned something of its Agony in the First World War.

CHAPTER 10

Activity in Peacetime

Two aspects of the service given by women during the First World War should not be forgotten. They neither had the vote nor, in the case of the Sisters, was their nursing status legally recognized. Even the word 'nurse' was not legally protected. Much was asked of women and they gave immeasurably more than could have been envisaged in 1914. Nearly two hundred QAs, their Reserve, and VADs died on Active Service between 1914 and 1918. Thirty-six were either killed or drowned. On 19 July, 1919, there was a Victory Parade through London, starting in Kensington Gardens and returning there two hours later. The nursing services all took part and were acclaimed by the crowds. Then the QAIMNS settled down to nursing the army in peacetime.

Although limited suffrage had been given to women in 1918, many of those who took part in the Victory Parade could not vote, for this franchise was denied to women of less than thirty years of age. Not until 1928 did women have equal voting rights with men.

In addition to the QAIMNS, QAIMNS (R) and VAD casualties of the war, there had been many in the TFNS. Their service was widely recognized, not least by Dame Maud McCarthy. The Territorial Force became the Territorial Army in 1920 and a year later the TFNS was reorganized into the Territorial Army Nursing Service, with Dame Maud as their Matron-in-Chief.

The QAIMNS continued to nurse the soldier, wherever he might be in those parts of the globe which used to be called 'red on the map' – the British Empire and its post-War Protectorates. They also nursed the families of the army. This they had done since 1902, but in a somewhat ill-organized way. In 1921 a sister service to the QAIMNS came into being, the Queen Alexandra's Military Families Nursing Service.

Although the Midwives Act (Great Britain), which provided that the title of midwife should not be used unless the woman was certified, had come into force in 1902, (and many members of the QAMFNS were midwives), the Nurses Act 'to provide for the Registration of Nurses for the Sick' did not become law until the end of 1919. The word 'nurse' had at last become protected.

The General Medical Council had been formed as early as 1858 for the protection of doctors and, indeed, their patients. Not until 1888 were the first demands for the registration of hospital nurses made: by 1914 they were becoming insistent, as were the demands for womens' suffrage.

Under the terms of the Act the General Nursing Council kept a register of all qualified nurses according to the details laid down by the General Nursing Council. These details had to be approved by the Minister of Health and the nurses whose names were registered had to have had experience for three years prior to the passing of the Act. The College of Nursing, Limited – which became the Royal College of Nursing in 1928 – had much to do with the passing of the Nurses Acts covering England and Wales and subsequently Scotland and Ireland, which protected the new State Registered Nurses.

It was appropriate that, in 1922, when the College decided to appoint a President, the first one should have been Dame Sidney Browne, who had had years of practical and administrative nursing experience, as well as being an initial organizer and the first Matron-in-Chief of the QAIMNS. By 1922 Dame Maud McCarthy had succeeded her as Matron-in-Chief of the TANS and thus the link between civil and military nursing was seen to be tangibly maintained. It was a connecting link which had been first seen in 1860, when Mrs Wardroper of St Thomas's, with Sarah Anne Terrot as her assistant, became the first Superintendent of The Nightingale School of Nursing.

There have continued to be many links between the QAs and civil nurses since the early years following the First World War, and one of the earliest was a Royal one. Queen Alexandra died in 1925, and Queen Mary succeeded her as President of the

QAIMNS in the following year. She became Patron of the College of Nursing in the same year and continued in that office when the College received its Royal Charter two years later. Queen Mary also became President of the QAIMNS (R) and TANS in 1926. Queen Alexandra had been much beloved by the QAs and she was intensely proud of them, taking a personal interest in their work and welfare. The same relationship was to be maintained between her daughter-in-law and the QAs.

The year 1926 was momentous for the Service. Not only did the QAs have a new President but their actual structure was altered. The first change was the absorption of Queen Alexandra's Military Nursing Service (India) into the Service. Until that date members of the QAIMNS had not served in India. At the beginning of the new absorption the members of both Services were interchangeable but, understandably, the members of QAMNS (India) felt they had been swallowed up. This feeling lasted for a comparatively short while and the absorption, or merger, was a smooth one. In 1929 there were a hundred and ninety-nine QAIMNS in India and nineteen QAMNS (India). By 1935 two hundred and eighty-eight QAIMNS were serving in India and there were only eight QAMNS (India). The post of Lady Superintendent in India disappeared and was replaced by that of Principal Matron and, later, Chief Principal Matron.

The title of Lady Superintendent had had a long and honourable life and it was sad to see it go, for it dated back to 1869. The title of Principal Matron also passed into history as far as military nursing is concerned when the QAs became a Corps, but the word 'Principal' is retained in civil nursing as a title for the higher grades of nursing administrator.

The year 1926 also saw the formation of the nursing service for the Indian Army, the Indian Military Nursing Service. The members of the IMNS were to see much service with the QAs in the years ahead.

A future Matron-in-Chief, Dame Monica Johnson, had joined the Families Service at the end of 1925, having done her midwifery training at the Louise Margaret Hospital as a paying pupil, and was delighted that, because of the forthcoming amalgamation, she was able to wear the famous and respected red cape.

The QAMFNS had been somewhat looked down upon by the regular QAs. This may have been partly due to the latter's well-known 'exclusiveness', whether merited or not, and perhaps it could be said that, to them, the younger sister Service presented a somewhat Mrs Gampish image, which was certainly not merited. This feeling of superiority passed with the amalgamation and, wearing their red capes, the Sisters who had exclusively nursed the families of the Army joined the *élite*, as the QAIMNS were, a trifle unkindly perhaps, sometimes called.

They had two far unkinder nicknames, neither of which were in the least bit merited but which, because they were (or were supposed to be) humorous, the QAs did not resent. One was 'Queer And Impossible, Mostly Not Sane' and the other 'Queer Assortment of Individuals, Mainly Non-Sexed'. Since the QAIMNS became a Corps those nicknames have passed into memory.

From 1926 onwards, the QAs were responsible for the nursing of the British and Indian armies and their wives and children, wherever they might be stationed. Although the QAs had had officer status before 1926 it was not until that year that they were granted equivalent rank with army officers. They had yet to hold commissions.

By 1927 the Regulations for Admission to the QAIMNS included the proviso that candidates had to have had three years training in a general hospital recognized by the General Nursing Council as a complete training school. They also had to be of 'pure European descent' and daughters of British parents. Preference was no longer given to daughters of officers of the armed services, although many of the candidates were officers' daughters.

In 1929 the British Army on the Rhine was evacuated and all the QAs were withdrawn from Germany. They had served there since 1918 and not until 1945 were they to nurse in Germany again.

There was a new Matron-in-Chief in 1930, Miss Marguerite Elizabeth Medforth. Her four-year appointment was marked by an event of great importance, one which is now taken for granted. The Minutes of the Nursing Board reveal that on 23 November, 1931, there was an amendment to the regulations regarding admission to the QAIMNS and TANS: henceforward candidates 'must be State Registered'. This involved their having to pass the necessary examinations as well as undergo hospital training. Now that the initials SRN are such an accepted fact by hospital patients it is curious to recall that until comparatively recently, many members of the QAIMNS did not have those initials after their names.

Miss Medforth's name, however, is not generally remembered because of the fact that she was Matron-in-Chief when entrants to the Service had to be State Registered. Instead it is recalled because she presented a tennis cup to the QAs, to be competed for annually. Not until after the Second World War did members of the Service see their Matron-in-Chief with any regularity. In fact, many of them only met her at their initial interview. Now there is an Annual Tennis Day as well as an Annual Sports' Day, at Aldershot, to both of which the Matron-in-Chief always goes and they are two of the many occasions when QAs have the opportunity of seeing her. At least some of the credit for this should be given to Miss Medforth. She retired in 1934 and was succeeded by Miss Daisy Maud Martin.

By the nineteen-thirties each big military hospital at home and overseas had its own QA Mess, presided over by the Matron. But before then there were QAs stationed in such places as the Crown Colonies of Hong Kong and Gibraltar and in many parts of the Middle and Far East, and they regularly served on troopships. The fact that they served wherever the army did, inevitably resulted in their experiences being varied indeed. They were in Khartoum, for instance, in 1925, when there was a mutiny among Sudanese troops and a number of the casualties were nursed by the RAMC and the QAIMNS.

In 1935 the QAs were called upon to assist in the relief of both civil and military casualties of natural disaster. On 31 May the town of Quetta, in North-West India, now part of Pakistan, was destroyed by an earthquake. Tented hospitals had to be erected at speed and QAs were summoned from many parts of India. The surgical and fracture cases among the Indian casualties were taken to the Mayo Hospital at Lahore and the treatment was later described as being like that of highly specialized fracture clinics in the United Kingdom or America.

Three QAs travelled to Lahore from Kasauli by train. One of them* wrote in a letter dated 6 June, 1933 to another QA.†

'A week tonight I was in the train bound for Lahore. We spent Saturday morning at Lahore Mess and at about 2 pm we and two from Lahore and one from Ambala started off from the Air Park on the Viceroy's plane . . . We had such a grand send off – even the Brigadier came down to wish us luck . . . We had rather a nasty trip as far as Multan as we got into a wind and dust storm . . . The RAMC colonel and some of the Leicester officers were so kind and took us to the nearest place where we could rest, which was a small ward of the IMH. We were given brandy and soda and ices so we soon bucked up. The temperature there was 120° so I have experienced real hot weather. By the time we had recovered and felt more like ourselves the pilot arrived and told us we had to stay the night at Multan . . . We were taken to the Officers' Mess for tea and had a grand time—they seemed to be thoroughly enjoying it all too as all the wives were in the hills. After tea we went to BMH . . . Then we were taken to the club for drinks and on to the Mess again for dinner. By this time all the officers in Multan seemed to have collected there . . . We left at 12 pm and had to get up at 4.30 am as the pilot wanted to start early. However, we didn't get off until 7 am owing to some mishap.

'Crossing the Sind Desert was wonderful. We were 14,000 feet up but all felt grand. Our excitement was over when we reached Quetta. Words can't describe the appearance of it from the air and when we landed it looked worse. It is a dreadful affair. We are hectic and I am on night duty in families with about 60 women. However, they are wasting no time in clearing the women out of Quetta . . . We still have tremors during the night which are very terrifying.'

Such flights marked the beginning of the era when QAs would

* The late Elsie Arnott (who subsequently married Captain Cawthorne).
† Mrs Irene Duncan.

go where they were needed by air. In 1935 that form of transport for them was unique. But it was not to be very long before casualties of war were to be taken from battle zones by air transport, tended by QAs. The Second World War was only four years away.

Almost exactly two years after the Quetta Earthquake a few QAs were to make another journey by air in response to an emergency call. This time they flew to Gibraltar from England. They went by seaplane, for the airstrip at Gibraltar had not then been built. The Spanish Civil War was in progress and the German battleship *Deutschland* was hit by two bombs while at anchor off Ibiza. There were approximately a hundred casualties, mostly due to burns which were complicated by wounds and fractures. *Deutschland* reached Gibraltar the following day, 30 May, 1937. Fifty-five of the most seriously hurt German sailors were taken to the Military Hospital. HMS *Hunter* had struck a mine near Almeria just over a fortnight earlier and HM Hospital Ship *Maine* had brought twenty casualties to Gibraltar on 15 May. They, too, were chiefly suffering from burns.

Casualties on this scale and of this type put a severe strain on the medical authorities in Gibraltar. At that time it was considered that cases of severe burns should each have a special nurse for the first forty-eight hours. Clearly this was impossible. But the QAs in Gibraltar did valiant work as did the local VADs and several Gibraltarian and other young women who had just been attending a course of St John Ambulance First Aid lectures. One of these described the QAs as being the 'heroines' of the period: 'They worked non-stop until the others [from England] arrived'. The same lady wrote: 'Lemon curd still turns me up a bit.' This was because of the many hours she spent in the hospital spreading ointment, closely resembling this substance, on lint with which to dress the wounds. The 'lemon curd' ointment was probably vaseline and eucalyptus which the RAMC found particularly beneficial among the casualties of *Deutschland*.

The work of the military and civilian hospital personnel did not go unrecognized and the German Government awarded them with varying classes of the German Red Cross. The decorations were presented after the incident on board one of *Deutschland*'s sister battleships by the German Admiral Commanding. The ladies who received them wore hats and gloves, and there was dancing – chiefly old-fashioned waltzes – under the awnings. The war which was soon to affect the dancers of both nationalities so greatly seemed very far away.

CHAPTER 11

The Second World War

WHEN the Second World War broke out on 3 September, 1939 the Matron-in-Chief at the War Office was Miss Roy. There were less than seven hundred regulars in the Service at that time. Under her guidance the Reserve and the TANS were mobilized at speed and merged into the QAIMNS. As had happened in 1914, within a few days a group of QAs sailed to France with the British Expeditionary Force. This time they took tin hats and gas masks with them.

The 'Phoney War' lasted until May 1940, and during that period the QAs in France had little to do in the way of nursing, for there was little fighting. There was also little sickness. The Tommy of 1939 was a physically fit man. The general health of the nation had greatly improved during the previous forty years and the health of the army had improved correspondingly.

During the First World War there had been a Matron-in-Chief in France and Flanders. In the Second a Principal Matron was in charge – Miss (later Dame Katharine) Jones. She had the equivalent rank of Lieutenant-Colonel under the orders of 1926 granting equivalent ranks. In 1940, after the evacuation from Dunkirk, she became Matron-in-Chief. A year later, in 1941, the QAs were granted Emergency Commissions, again with equivalent ranks, and she became a Brigadier.

Miss Jones was responsible for the QAs during the German advance through the Low Countries and the resulting retreat and evacuation of the British. The QAs nursed the troops and refugees during the trek to the coast. That all of them returned to England from different ports in France was part of the miracle remembered as Dunkirk. The first six QAs had landed at Cherbourg on 10 September, 1939. Well over a thousand (including, of course, Reserves and TANS) returned in June 1940.

No 11 General Hospital, which had been formed at Netley in 1939, served at Le Havre. Its equipment was destroyed and when it returned to England from Cherbourg it brought back one typewriter. It was all that was left.

The list of places in which QAs served during the Second World War is, inevitably, a far longer one than that of the First World War. In October 1939, No 12 General Hospital was formed. It was the first medical unit to go to the Middle East during the war. The QAs, like those who had gone to France with the BEF, were issued with tin hats. They called them Battle Bowlers and painted them a dull shade of yellow when they wore them in the desert. They travelled by way of Southampton and Cherbourg and then by train to Marseilles. From there they went to Haifa, and once in Palestine some of the QAs stayed in Haifa, some went to India and some to Jerusalem.

Those in Jerusalem nursed, in the Spring of 1940, casualties of the Syrian Campaign, both Free and Vichy French. Tragically their duties included keeping those patients apart.

In 1941 some of the QAs who had left England with No 12 General Hospital were sent from Jerusalem to the Suez Canal where their patients included Germans, Italians and Free French – all wounded in the Western Desert. And from there, in April 1942, they went to Tobruk by hospital ship. They were greeted in the harbour by a German air raid.

The hospital in which they worked was in an Italian barracks. It had been shelled and bombed and blankets were hung where doors and windows had been in an attempt to give protection against the frequent sandstorms.

The dive-bombing which had greeted the QAs continued. The drinking water ration was three-quarters of a pint a day and the number of casualties, both British and German, increased. Inevitably there was a shortage of equipment which ranged from beds for the patients to surgical gloves.

Throughout this period the QAs were wearing their grey and scarlet cotton dresses and red capes. They also wore their white veil caps, replacing them with Battle Bowlers when there was an air raid in progress, which was the case more often than not.

Laundry facilities were minimal and they washed themselves and their clothes, when they could, in buckets of sea water.

When it became apparent that Tobruk would fall to the Germans it was decided to take the QAs to the base at Alexandria. It was not a decision they took themselves nor, indeed, wanted taken for them. They went overland, driven by an American Field Ambulance Unit, to Mersa Matruh, where for the first time for many weeks they were able to swim and wash in the sea, and then on to Alexandria. Tobruk fell within a few days and the QAs were not among the prisoners of war.

A very different situation obtained in the Far East.

There had been dancing on board *Deutschland* in Gibraltar in 1937. In those pre-war days there was also dancing in the International Settlement in Shanghai; but of course the QAs stationed in Shanghai worked as well as danced. The British Military Hospital had about sixty beds; but, once diagnosed, smallpox and cholera patients were sent to the civilian isolation hospital.

The Sino-Japanese War had escalated sharply in 1937 and, by 1938, the Japanese were occupying the Chinese part of Shanghai. British sentries were posted at one end of Garden Bridge, separating it from the International Settlement, and Japanese at the other. The temporary postponement of the Second World War achieved at Munich lasted eleven months, during which time many believed the Japanese Army to be 'bogged in China', as the catch-phrase of the period was. When the war in Europe began, an International Guard patrolled the International Settlement at night. The Italian marines remained in the patrol after Italy declared war on the Allies in June 1940. The QAs were quartered in the sector of the Settlement which was guarded by these marines, with whom they were technically at war.

Such protection was not to last for long, for in August, 1940, the British troops were withdrawn from Shanghai. The officers and men went to Singapore, the wives and children to Australia; some of the QAs, of whom there were six in Shanghai, went to Singapore. The Matron, Miss C. L. M. West, was later killed at sea.

14. 'On 19 July, 1919 there was a Victory Parade through London.' QAs pass the saluting base outside Buckingham Palace, watched by George V, Queen Mary and Queen Alexandra.

15. Queen Mary with members of the Service of which she was President.

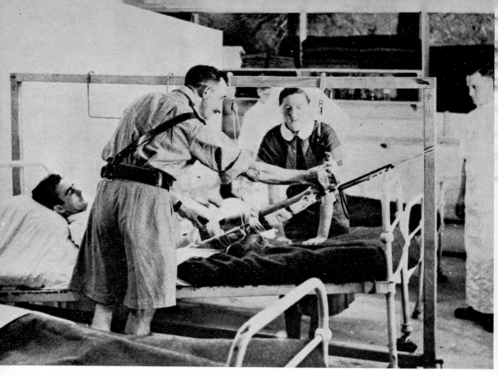

16. *A portable X-Ray in North Africa during the Second World War. This photograph was taken before the QAs went into khaki.*

17. *A QA tending a helpless patient in a tented hospital during the Second World War. 'Not until 1942 were the sisters in the Western Desert and North Africa allowed to wear khaki slacks and battle blouses.'*

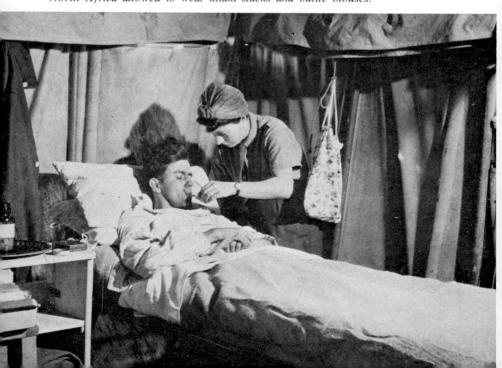

18. *QAs visit the Pyramids while stationed in Egypt during the Second World War.*

19. *The Depot, QAIMNS at Anstie Grange, Holmwood, Surrey, on 8 June, 1948. Queen Mary is flanked by the Matron-in-Chief, Dame Louisa Wilkinson and Lt-Gen Sir Neil Cantlie. A future Matron-in-Chief is also in the photograph, 'Junior Instructor Cozens', the second from the right in the front row.*

20. *The Colonel-in-Chief, Princess Margaret, Countess of Snowdon presenting an Army Trained Nurse Certificate to Staff Sergeant J. Grimshaw on 16 May, 1963, having laid the foundation stone of the QARANC Training Centre, Aldershot, earlier in the day. The Matron-in-Chief, Dame Barbara Cozens is standing next to her.*

Miss K. M. Thomson went to Australia, but her next posting was to Hong Kong where she was when the Colony fell to the Japanese, less than three weeks after they had entered the war, on Christmas Day, 1941. She and her surviving colleagues, together with the rest of the garrison, became prisoners-of-war. It was the first time QAs had been POWs: they were to remain in captivity in Hong Kong for three years and eight months.

For a while at the beginning of that period they continued to nurse the troops at the two military hospitals, Bowen Road and St Albert's. Miss Thomson was Matron of the latter and Miss E. M. B. Dyson of the former. St Albert's was then moved to St Theresa's, where they continued to nurse British troops. In August, 1942, the QAs were all moved to the Civilian Camp at Stanley, there to nurse in the civilian hospital at Tweed Bay.

The conditions in which they worked were unique by reason of their captivity. They behaved like the officers whose relative rank they had and, as the good nurses that they were, displayed courage, self-sacrifice and care for those in their charge. But they were not part of the army, for all their relative rank, and thus the behaviour – or misbehaviour – of their captors under the rules of the Geneva Convention did not apply in their case. George VI had given his approval for QAs to wear their relative rank badges on 30 April, 1941 (their President, Queen Mary, had consented on 15 March), but the badges had not reached Hong Kong when the QAs fell into Japanese hands. Indeed, when Miss Thomson's Commanding Officer introduced her to a Japanese Colonel and showed him her red cape (of which there were few left by that time, for their possessions were minimal after the shelling) and said she ranked as a Major in the British Army, the Japanese merely laughed. Since the Japanese nurses were known as the Sisters of Joy, although the QAs there gave them the 'title' of Comfort Corps, the idea that the British Army Sisters should have officer rank and status was inconceivable.

One of the disadvantages of not being regarded as military personnel was the fact that the QAs received no pay in captivity, although a little money from the Red Cross did get through.

Soon after the outbreak of hostilities Miss Thomson was

wounded and another regular QA, Brenda Morgan, was killed by the same shell. Mary Currie, who was Home Sister at Bowen Road, acted as Matron at St Albert's in Miss Thomson's place. When the war was over a letter reached the Secretary of State for War from the Nursing Detachment of the Hong Kong Volunteer Defence Corps commending Miss Currie's 'coolness, leadership and bravery' which had so greatly contributed to the high state of morale. There were thirty-six signatures.

Two Canadian Sisters of the Royal Canadian Army Medical Corps, Miss K. G. Christie and Miss A. M. Waters, had gone to Hong Kong with the Canadian troops in October 1941. In September 1943 they were repatriated, together with other Canadian civilians from all over the Far East whom the Americans agreed to include in the repatriation. These two Canadians worked and suffered and made friends with the QAs in the Bowen Road Hospital and then in Stanley Camp. They had been given names and addresses of many relatives and friends of the internees and POWs before they left. These had to be memorized since the Japanese did not allow them to take any written material with them. They tore up the lists just before being searched by the Japanese and then re-wrote them from memory as soon as possible. When they reached Goa they were transferred to MS *Gripsholm* and on board began writing letters, which were mailed from Port Elizabeth, their first stop on the way back to Canada. Among the letters written was one to Dame Katharine Jones at the War Office which included Miss Dyson's report on the condition of the QAs. The report was succinct and, though long, had all been committed to memory. It made awesome reading. The QAs and their relatives owed much to those two Canadian Sisters.

No such news reached home from another part of the Far East. It had been planned to open a Military Families Hospital in Singapore, but in 1940 it was decided to abandon the project. Therefore the original thirty-three QAs destined for Singapore were reduced to twenty-five. The lives of eight British women may well have been spared by that decision. The unlucky twenty-five left England in July. Among them was Miss V. M. E. Jones, destined to be Principal Matron, Malaya Command. She was one of the four QA Matrons to lose their lives, being among the QAs and other nurses who died when the ship, *Kuala*, was bombed by the Japanese leaving Singapore in February 1942.

In March, 1941, an Indian Army Infantry battalion and a Combined General Hospital sailed together from Bombay to Singapore. There were sixteen Indian Nursing Sisters of the IMNS on board and eight QAs. Of the latter one was to become Matron-in-Chief and, like so many before her, a Dame of the British Empire. Her name was Margot Turner.

The story of the surrender of Singapore to the Japanese is a pathetic one. It is also, like so many stories concerning the British Army and those who nursed them, a story of high heroism.

After their lightning advance down the Malayan Peninsula, the Japanese landed on Singapore Island on 9 February, 1942, having earlier subjected the city to heavy aerial bombardment. Although many women and children had already gone, there was still a great number left and a boat was earmarked to take away as many of them as possible on the 11th. It was decided that half the QAs and half the IMNS would go, together with all the VADs. Miss Jones asked for volunteers. They all wanted to stay. She therefore had the unenviable task of deciding herself who would go and who would stay. The ship, *Empire Star*, duly sailed from the flaming harbour and was bombed and hit before reaching Batavia. The survivors eventually reached Ceylon, Australia or India.

On board *Empire Star* the Australian Sisters were accommodated on the port side of the for'ard hold, and the QAs and the VADs on the starboard. The lights failed and it was completely dark on the starboard side. There was only one lavatory, in the main part, and there was a constant queue outside it. During the waves of bombing it was found to be slightly less alarming in the hold where one could be certain to be among known friends, even though, when there were near-misses, the bombs burst at ear level. One of the VADs on board recalls being fully aware at the time of a feeling of gratitude for being with trained women, referring, of course, to the QAs. They were so 'un-hysterical'.

Once in Java, where they were not expected, they had a six hour wait before being taken to a Roman Catholic Convent School where 'the QAs got organized and had a hospital running and operations being performed in no time'.

Two days after *Empire Star*'s departure from Singapore *Kuala* sailed. The remaining QAs were ordered, in some cases at under an hour's notice, to go in her. Some news of the treatment nurses had received in Hong Kong had filtered through. While it was yet possible to get them out of Singapore the question of allowing them to stay did not arise, except in their own minds. They had not, after all, joined the Service to leave their patients as they were now being ordered to do.

Kuala sailed in the evening. One QA was killed in an air raid as they were waiting to board her. Early the following morning she lay to off a small island called Pompong while some of the men on board went ashore to try and find branches with which to camouflage the ship. *Kuala*, although crowded with women and children, was very small. This attempt to gain a modicum of safety ended in tragedy for, while lying at anchor, a Japanese bomber scored a direct hit.

There were some fifty nursing Sisters on board, including the four Matrons who were killed, not all of them QAs. Few of them survived the direct hit, but of those who did some managed to land and ultimately reach Sumatra. There some were rescued. Others were interned later in the year when the Japanese occupied the whole island. Many were drowned, others died as the result of dive-bombing and machine-gunning, or later as POWs.

A small group of eight QAs with about two hundred and fifty women and children, after a precarious existence on Pompong, were given the opportunity of leaving on board a small steamer, *Tanjong Penang*. Of those eight QAs, the ones to leave were the Sisters who were off duty at the time; those who were on duty remained – to face what then appeared to be almost certain death. They had all been nursing the sick and wounded, with none of the tools or comforts of their profession, and had organized themselves into a rota. Of the QAs who sailed in *Tanjong Penang* to nurse the wounded who were on board as

well as to help care for the women and children, only Margot
Turner survived.

During the night following the crowded ship's sailing she was
bombed and the casualties were extremely heavy. One of them
was Beatrice Le Blanc Smith, a regular QA. She had written
home on 1 January, 1942, from 1st Malaya General Hospital.
The letter reached England on 1 May, by which time, unknown
to her family, she was already dead. In 1945 her stepmother
copied out part of the letter and sent it to the Matron-in-Chief,
then Dame Louisa Wilkinson. The last sentence read: 'At last
my existence here seems about to be justified and the year of
"fun and games" preceding this was just the prelude and will
be something to be remembered with a tolerant smile.'

Beatrice Le Blanc Smith was with Margot Turner in the sea.
They managed to tie two small rafts together, and they picked up
fourteen people, six of them children. There was not room for all
of them on the raft and they clung to its sides. Miss Le Blanc
Smith was already wounded but insisted on being among those
in the water until Miss Turner hauled her up on to the raft the
next morning. She died later in the day. Her own description
of the last year of her life and her attitude to it as well as the
manner of her death are typical of the high standard that the
QAIMNS set itself.

The women and children died on the raft or slipped away from
it to death in the sea until, on the third day, only Margot Turner
was left. She was rescued by a Japanese battleship on the fourth
day. While the American-trained, English-speaking doctor on
board undoubtedly saved her life at that time, rescue did not
mean release from suffering. There followed three years in
captivity in the Dutch East Indies in more than one prison camp,
years of hardship, illness, loneliness, grief, hunger, hard work –
and friendship.

When it was all over she wrote to the Matron-in-Chief on 25
October, 1945, 'having arrived home last night,' offering to come
to London to give such details as she knew of the fate of other
QAs who had sailed in both *Kuala* and *Tanjong Penang*. At
the beginning of November Dame Louisa gave her the addresses

of the next-of-kin of the casualties. News of the missing from Singapore had indeed taken a long time to reach England.

By the end of the summer of 1945 the Second World War was over and the QAs were coming home. At the outbreak of war they had been stationed in Gibraltar, Malta, Burma, China, Egypt, Palestine and India as well as the military hospitals in the United Kingdom.

In Gibraltar during the war a hospital was made in an underground cavern over a thousand feet high. The patients were all in bunks to save space.

Malta was given the George Cross by King George VI in 1942 for the island's fortitude during the siege and the bombing. The QAs there shared in the award with the citizens and members of the Armed Forces. Apart from the bombing, severe food rationing and shortage of medical supplies made their lives difficult as well as dangerous. Indeed, Malta was among the places where, at periods, operations had to be performed without gloves. The main military hospital was alongside the aerodrome and the other two were near military targets of importance. They were bombed accordingly and the QAs at the Families Hospital did sterling work for Maltese women and their infants during such raids. An epidemic of poliomyelitis in 1943 in Malta increased even further the hazards of the beleaguered island.

The war also took QAs to the primitive and dangerous conditions prevalent in West and East Africa and Abyssinia, and to Burma via India. They all quickly learned to bear with the heat, the snakes and the animals which came unpleasantly close to the tented wards and sleeping quarters at night. They wore bush jackets and khaki drill slacks or monsoon boots and trench mackintoshes. In the heat and the rain they nursed the wounded from the campaign in the Arakan and those sick with the unfamiliar diseases of the jungle. The bamboo- and grass-thatched wards with their mud floors were not ideal for nursing but the nurses improvised and the patients of the Fourteenth Army were made as comfortable as possible.

In England clothes rationing was such that by November 1942, there was the greatest difficulty in obtaining the scarlet and grey material for QAs' walking out uniform and the Board of Trade suggested that khaki be adopted. The Nursing Board informed the Board of Trade that 'they would view with great disquiet any alterations, and would be prepared to accept such a change only as a most urgent wartime measure and in case of the materials becoming unavailable'. Queen Mary herself expressed her dislike of the idea except when extreme necessity demanded it.

Practicality prevailed and in 1943 the change to the khaki uniform as worn by officers of the ATS was authorized. It was to be worn as from 1 January, 1944. Soon afterwards the QAs were wearing scarlet and grey lanyards on the khaki uniforms, and their special identity was thus preserved. By 1944 no more white tropical dress was issued; khaki drill was also the outfit for those serving in hot climates. In January 1943, a grey uniform peaked cap had been put into production to take the place of the brimmed hats in which somewhat schoolgirlish headwear they had gone to war in 1939.

At Tobruk the Sisters had worn grey dresses. In West Africa in 1943 they were wearing white tropical dresses and cumbersome thigh-length white canvas mosquito boots. The slacks worn in Burma were far more comfortable and practical. Not until 1942 were the Sisters in the Western Desert and North Africa allowed to wear khaki slacks and battle blouses. The unsuitable clothing which the Sisters in Tobruk had worn in the spring of 1942 undoubtedly made everything more difficult for them while they were nursing and travelling back across the desert. And many QAs had already found out for themselves the unsuitability of wearing dresses on active service when attending to stretcher cases in Belgium and France in the early part of the war. After Tobruk the authorities in Cairo recognized the disadvantages of dresses for the nurses who were to travel across the desert in lorries and ambulance cars.

The QAs who went with the army in 1944 to Anzio, on the west coast of Italy, were equipped for the occasion with battle-dress. The beachhead was under constant bombardment and there was a seemingly endless procession of stretcher cases being brought to the ten-acre field, packed with the tents of the

Casualty Clearing Station. The QAs were landed by tender from a hospital ship. They had to sleep in slit trenches, two shovel lengths long, one length deep and one wide. They dived into these when off duty for protection from shellfire and bombing. The wards were dug in too, and covered with tenting. QAs were among the many casualties of the battle at Anzio. The fact that women were there, sharing the hazards of the front line had an inspiriting effect on the morale of all involved in the landing, quite apart from the fact that they gave invaluable nursing assistance to the sorely tried RAMC. Their motto of *Sub Cruce Candida* remained but at Anzio they had, of necessity, an additional one. It was *Dig or Die*.

By 1945 QAs had served, apart from those places already mentioned, in Norway and in Iceland, in Greece and the Dodecanese, in Ceylon, in South Africa and, of course in the Normandy Landing of 1944 and the Battle of the Rhine where, as at Anzio, they wore their battledress in battle conditions. They had even taken part in the invasion of Madagascar in 1942, working on board a hospital ship to which the casualties were taken.

They had served in hospital trains and hospital ships, and had lost their lives in both. They had been bombed in England too. At no time, from the cessation of the Phoney War, had the life of any of them been cushy.

The pre-war 'exclusiveness' of the Regulars had been eroded: the QAs were too busy to notice who wore red capes and who wore grey ones. Each had depended upon the other.

In 1945 the Matron-in-Chief made an extensive tour of medical units in the British Liberation Army in North-West Europe and in her report stated that many Matrons 'spoke appreciatively of their experienced VADs and grieved that they had not taken up nursing as a profession'. It had all been a team effort. The QAs (No regulars were taken on during the war and so they were far outnumbered by the Reserves.) had worked as one part of the team with the TANS, VADs and the IMNS. At the outbreak of war there had been fifty-five members of the IMNS; by 1945 two hundred QAs had been diverted to nurse Indian troops.

21. *'The first Gurkha recruits enlisted in Singapore, were brought to England and arrived at Queen Alexandra Camp in November, 1962.'*

22. *'Princess Margaret opened the Royal Pavilion on 17 October, 1967. Dame Barbara Cozens had by this time become Colonel Commandant and Dame Margot Turner was Matron-in-Chief.'*

23. *Badges of the past and the badge of the present. Left to right: Princess Christian's Army Nursing Service Reserve, Queen Alexandra's Imperial Military Nursing Service, Queen Alexandra's Imperial Military Nursing Service Reserve, Territorial Army Nursing Service, Queen Alexandra's Military Families Nursing Service, Queen Alexandra's Royal Army Nursing Corps.*

24. *QARANC Training Centre, The Royal Pavilion, Aldershot. '. . . it has an air of elegance as well as practicality.' The round foundation stone can be seen on the right of the photograph.*

The RAMC and the Army Dental Corps, which had come into being in 1921 and was to become Royal in 1946, comprised the other parts of the medical team. The nursing services had learned with their brother medical services the value of speedy evacuation of the wounded and knew that the regular flights from Northern France taking the casualties to England towards the end of the war were as much the life-savers as the bombers had been the killers of the Second World War.

They had learned too of the enormous benefits of sulphonamide drugs, the Army Blood Transfusion Service and penicillin. They had seen that early surgery, antibiotics, mepacrine tablets and the use of DDT as well as inoculations had all helped to contain the casualty rate. They had served in Mobile Surgical Teams and had served in, as well as behind, the battle areas. They had nursed jungle sores and dengue, desert sores, smallpox and VD as well as every kind of wound. They had nursed German, Italian and Japanese prisoners-of-war. They had nursed refugees and nationals of every country in which they had served. They had nursed the British Army, for which purpose they had joined the Service; and they had nursed one another.

It had all been very sordid and very depressing. At times it had been very dangerous indeed. For some it was exciting. For others it had been a time of adventure and new experience and rare friendships, to be looked back on with a certain pride – even, by some, with nostalgia. For many it had meant death, illness, bereavement and great loneliness. For others the war was a mixture of fear and fortitude. The Second World War had meant too that seldom mentioned but highly distressing malady, homesickness.

Such were the many facets of the war in which QAs had taken such a varied and encompassing part. They had seen every kind of bestiality, every kind of wound, both to the body and to the mind and, not least, to the spirit. Perhaps the epitome of it all they saw at the very end, in the Spring of 1945 in Germany – at a place called Belsen.

G

CHAPTER 12

QAIMNS: The Last Years

THE Concentration Camp of Belsen was liberated by the British in April, 1945. Vast numbers of human beings had been exterminated there by the Nazis in conditions of unparalleled horror. The RAMC and the QAs who went with them found a situation there which, had they not seen it for themselves, they would have considered impossible even during the most devastating war the world had known. Others, including a group of Members of Parliament, saw the horrors, but the Medical Services had to do something about them, and at once.

The first medical appreciation was written twenty-four hours after the first contact with the Camp on 18 April. It mentioned two camps. Camp I was hutted and held approximately twenty-two thousand females and eighteen thousand males. The nationalities were mixed but were mostly Poles and Russians. The huts were of the size used in the British Army to house thirty men; in one alone eleven hundred people were found. There were no beds, no blankets and in most cases no clothes. There was no sanitation. There were piles of corpses in various stages of decomposition. The initial estimate was that there were approximately eight thousand dead. Later this estimate was revised, for many bodies were found in the huts among the barely living. They were chiefly suffering from typhus, TB and disorders due to starvation such as oedema, and they were covered in lice. The stench was nauseous.

In Camp II the conditions were slightly better; the buildings were made of brick. Six hundred men were housed in a building designed for one hundred and fifty.

The first action to be taken was to bury the dead, burn the excreta, clean the buildings and move the occupants of Camp I to Camp II. By 21 April, 'in the light of experience to date', diet sheets were made out for the fit and the unfit. There were few of the former.

Amongst the appalling difficulties with which the medical services had to contend was the fact that many of the internee doctors and nurses were incapable of helping without the closest supervision. The terrible conditions under which they had lived had made them apathetic and, having been starved, they would scrounge food, including that of their patients. As time went on the inadequacy of most of these internee medical staff was further realized: apart from their sickness and general debility it was apparent that their moral values had been destroyed by Belsen. This is evident from a report written on 10 May, which also stated that German medical aid had arrived and helped considerably. By then, too, a British General Hospital had come (there was already an augmented Casualty Clearing Station) and a Field Ambulance. The report stated that Field Ambulances are ideal 'where initiative, drive and improvization are essential requirements'.

It was not only in Belsen that QAs brought nursing expertise: they, with the RAMC, performed a similar and less publicized task of relief work at the camp at Sandbostel which was taken by the British a fortnight after Belsen. There, as at Belsen, they saw death and life in conditions of the utmost degradation and they used the same technique of the 'human laundry' to clean the inmates. Hundreds were hosed clean daily, shaved and sprayed with DDT and taken, in a blanket and by stretcher, to an improvised hospital.

The German forces surrendered to the Allies on 7 May, 1945. The war in the Far East dragged on for another three months until, after two atom bombs had been dropped on two major Japanese cities, that country surrendered on 14 August. There continued to be a flow of volunteers to join the QAIMNS (R) during those months, and afterwards, many of them specifically wanted to go to the Far East.

The name of a house in Surrey was to become increasingly familiar to QAs from then on – Anstie Grange. It had been taken over earlier in the war and was a holding unit and a depot in

1945. It was of particular use to those wishing to go to the Far East and for whom it was not possible to provide a period in a military hospital at home first. Anstie Grange was where those going overseas received lectures on what their duties would be in military hospitals, as well as being given the necessary inoculations and uniforms. QAs already in the Service went to Anstie Grange too, prior to new overseas postings. They no longer went abroad as part of a unit as they had done when the war started, but were sent individually as situations demanded. The double function of Anstie Grange was an important one and was indicative of the post-war reorganization to come.

To appreciate the difference Anstie Grange made to the QAs from 1945 onwards, reference should be made to the pre-war system of entry into the Service. Before the war, once a QA had passed her medical and been accepted by a Selection Board at the War Office in Whitehall, at which the Matron-in-Chief was generally present, she was given the name of a military hospital and the date on which she was to report there. It was at that hospital that she had to learn, by working, how different were the disciplines and practices of a military hospital from those in which she had trained and worked hitherto. It was fairly common in those days in the nineteen-twenties and thirties for a new QA to be the only one reporting for duty in a specific hospital, an experience as intimidating as for a child to be the only new pupil on the first day of term. The military terminology was strange to the new QA of that period, however experienced a trained nurse she might be, and the standards required by the QAIMNS were very high.

One such girl, for instance, on her first day on duty in a military hospital, where she was put in charge of a ward, saw that one of her patients was in urgent need of a doctor. She immediately sent for the doctor on duty. The orderlies on the ward then told her she should have sent for the Orderly Officer. The new QA thus learned her first lesson in military nomenclature and the patient received the medical attention required.

At the beginning of the war the system was changed and

members of the Reserve joined their hospitals in groups of a dozen or more.

At Anstie Grange, later in the war, the new QAs began to learn, through lectures, the rudiments of military practice, as opposed to having to absorb it gradually through experience in the wards. If the regulars among the Matrons in the first years of the war were considered to be stern ladies, theirs was a stern task, welding together into a harmonious whole a group of Reserves who had come from different civil hospitals and were accustomed to their own particular customs and practices. That they were able to do this in their varied wartime conditions is everlastingly to their credit.

Anstie Grange held its first Officers' Training Course in the spring of 1945 and became the Training Centre as well as the Depot in that year. But even after it had been in existence for some years, difficulties as regards military terminology could still arise. A newly-joined QA on a surgical ward in the early post-war period found a note reading 'S.U.S.' at the foot of the bed of one of her patients. He had a broken ankle and as far as she knew that was all that was wrong with him. However, following the practice of the hospital at which she had trained she saved a urine sample. Tests revealed nothing sinister, and the QA learned that her patient was a Soldier under Sentence.

The ATS had originally extended their Officers' Training Course at Windsor to include a selection of QAs, but after the first OTC course at Anstie Grange, the beginnings of general army procedure were learnt and, perhaps even more demandingly, taught there. The QAs began to learn how to salute and drill as well as such things as Military Law, documentation, discipline, obligations and traditions.

By 1946 the Nursing Board knew that it would not be long before the Matron-in-Chief would also be the Director of Army Nursing Services. The conception leading to the 'paper birth' of Queen Alexandra's Royal Army Nursing Corps had taken place. The gestation period had begun.

Anstie Grange had two different types of intake during the

years immediately following the Second World War: new QAs went there, so did experienced ones sent on special courses.

By 1948 the Depot had moved to a section of the Army School of Health at Mytchett, and the following year, on 1 February, the QAIMNS became the QARANC.

Prior to this happy event, for that is what indeed it was, it was already being mooted that there should be QAs not of officer rank. The Service had hitherto been composed entirely of those of officer status. The discussion was to last from 1945 until 1950. It was a novel idea, for, even though the Second World War had dispelled the feeling of exclusiveness peculiar to their Service, the QAs never lost their awareness of their relative ranks.

There was the much quoted episode which had taken place during the war, before the QAs went into khaki, of how a Principal Matron with the relative rank of Lt-Colonel was told by a liftman in a London hotel to wait while he took 'the lady officer up'. The young woman was an ATS subaltern. Proud though the QAs were of their scarlet and grey, khaki had brought at least one compensation other than practicality in the field.

Before the Depot and Training Establishment at Anstie Grange moved to Mytchett a Drumhead Service was held there, on 8 June, 1948. Queen Mary was present. She had agreed privately in February of that year to be Colonel-in-Chief of the new QARANC (to which title she had also given her approval) instead of her existing title of President. In fact she was to become Commandant-in-Chief when the Service became a Corps because for the first year of the Corps' existence the QAs were given the ranks used by the new Women's Royal Army Corps. Not until 1950 were army ranks used; then Queen Mary did become Colonel-in-Chief and Dame Anne Thomson, Matron-in-Chief and DANS, ceased being a Senior Controller and became the first nurse to be gazetted a Brigadier into the Regular British Army. Dame Katharine Jones had held that rank too, but hers had been an Emergency Commission.

At that Drumhead Service the DGAMS, Lt-Gen Sir Neil Cantlie, spoke of the service the QAs had given in the past to the Army and of the changes ahead. He approved of the fact that the QAs were extending and improving their own organization, however much 'mere man' might regret the fact that good nurses were turning to duties of administration. He warned them to keep their feminine characteristics in bringing sympathy and tenderness in pain and suffering and said: 'The hard boiled nurse or the battle-axe may have a role in the administrative and company side: she has no place in the ward.'

The warning was accepted, but to lose their femininity had never been the aim of the QAs. At the beginning of its life the military aspect of the new Corps may have been overstressed, but since they did much of their training and discipline themselves, while gratefully acknowledging initial help from the new WRAC and also the RAMC, this was not surprising. When, in 1950, they were given the same ranks as the rest of the army they did not forget that men had given them these ranks; they had not asked for them. In spite of the changes in the QAIMNS, so soon to become the QARANC, during the late nineteen-forties the members of the Service did not try to ape the men, nor have they done so since. No QA Mess, for all its army basis, is masculine in tone: femininity was and remains the essence of the Headquarters and other Messes.

Sir Neil, on that day in June, 1948, also suggested that QAs should have their own tune as a March Past while on parade, as had the RAMC. He made the suggestion that they should have 'Her bright smile haunts me still', and concluded his address with the words: 'Remember, above all, that the key to your popularity and the admiration you inspire rests upon your nursing of the sick and wounded.'

Professional nurses the QAs already were. Professional soldiers they were to become. That order of precedence remains the correct order of importance in their own eyes a quarter of a century later in that now doubly professional body, the QARANC.

While the planning for the new Corps was taking place Queen Mary continued to take an active and personal interest. She, through her Private Secretary, and Dame Louisa Wilkinson (the Matron-in-Chief from 1944 until 1948) corresponded at some length and a month after the Drumhead Service at Anstie Grange, Dame Louisa raised the matter of future Matrons-in-Chief having a King's Honorary title in accordance with long established military tradition.

George VI, understandably, did not care for one of the suggested titles, King's Honorary Nurse. Another idea was King's Honorary Director of Nursing. Dame Louisa herself did not like King's Honorary Nursing Sister, writing 'it is our lowest rank'. But Sister had always been an honourable form of address and was endeared to the army as well as to civilian patients, and in due course Dame Anne Thomson carried the initials KHNS after her name, and Dame Helen Gillespie, who succeeded her as Matron-in-Chief in 1952, the year of George VI's death, became the Queen's Honorary Nursing Sister.

This correspondence between Queen Mary and Dame Louisa lasted almost until the Matron-in-Chief's retirement. When she retired Dame Louisa became President of the Royal College of Nursing. She was the only ex-Matron-in-Chief, other than Dame Sydney Browne, to hold that appointment. Dame Sydney was unique in that she was not only the first President of the College but had been the first Matron-in-Chief. The long-established link between military and civil nursing was thus tightly maintained by Dame Louisa, on the eve of the QAIMNS becoming part of the British Army proper.

CHAPTER 13

Queen Alexandra's Royal Army Nursing Corps

O N 1 February, 1949, Dame Anne Thomson sent Queen Mary a telegram on behalf of the new Corps, greeting her as Commandant-in-Chief. The Queen Mother was delighted, but regretted that the Press had called her Commander-in-Chief in the newspapers, under the section of Royal Appointments. She also sent a telegram of greeting to the Corps.

The Matron-in-Chief gratefully acknowledged the greetings on behalf of the Corps and regretted the error in the Commandant-in-Chief's title in the Press, which was due to a typing error. Happily this had not occurred in AMD 4, the Army Medical Department which the Matron-in-Chief headed.

Since 1948, 27 March has been kept as QA Day, although the date of the 'paper birth' was 1 February. The date of the Royal Warrant signed by the husband of their first President whose name they still bear is the one the QAs chose as their own, and it is marked by services in military hospital chapels in the United Kingdom and wherever QAs are stationed abroad.

On QA Day an 'In Memoriam' notice appears in *The Times* which reads: 'QA Day. March 27th. On this day all members of Queen Alexandra's Royal Army Nursing Corps remember with pride and gratitude all comrades who gave their lives in the service of their country. *Sub Cruce Candida.*'

Such is the modern delight in initials that many people called, indeed still call, the nursing Sisters 'Quarancs'. But the QAs have never liked this. QAs they have been and QAs they remain – a convenient abbreviation perhaps, but a respectful as well as an affectionate one. Red Capes has also been a respectful term of endearment since the South African War.

The suggestion made by Sir Neil Cantlie in 1948 that the QAs should have a special tune as a March Past had been put into effect by 20 February, 1950, when Dame Anne Thomson wrote and offered to arrange for an RAMC band to come to London and play it specially for Queen Mary. But, glad though Queen Mary was that her Corps had a March of their own, she instructed her Private Secretary to inform the Matron-in-Chief that there could be no question of the RAMC band coming specially to play it for her. The tune, appropriately named 'Grey and Scarlet', was in fact played for the first time in public on 13 September, 1950, on the occasion of the new QARANC Depot and Training Establishment being opened at Hindhead. This had originally been built by the Canadians and named Ontario Camp: on that day it was appropriately renamed Queen Alexandra Camp.

'Grey and Scarlet' had been arranged by Capt Brown, Director of Music, RAMC, and consists of Purcell's 'King Arthur', followed by the traditional air 'Gentle Maiden'. The martial music followed by a peaceful melody signifies the dual role of the QA: part of the army, yet always a nurse.

On that cold and windy day the new Corps flag was flown for the first time, the red, white and blue colours, as originally chosen by Queen Alexandra for the ribbon to hold her badge, in nine horizontal stripes of varying widths forming a background to the new Corps badge. The badge was almost identical to the one designed by Queen Alexandra; the motto was the same; the name of the Service was different.

The long period when the QAs had been an 'officers only' body was over when, in July 1950, the first non-commissioned ranks were admitted into the Corps. The officers of the Depot presented the first one, Pte A. Catherall, number 0/100001, with a clock as a memento of the official opening of the new Depot and Training Establishment. It was an important occasion indeed: the Dedication Service was taken by the Chaplain General, Canon F. L. Hughes, and the Adjutant-General, Gen Sir James Steele, carried out the inspection and declared the Depot open and announced the new name of the camp.

It was the culmination of all the planning and paper work which had preceded the birth of the new Corps. Of the many

QARANC officers on parade that day, two had spent over three years as POWs. They had thus been out of touch with medical and nursing developments during that period. That they had accepted the fact that the years which the locusts had eaten had been given back to them and had used those years abundantly and to full measure was evidenced by the fact that one of them was the Commandant of Queen Alexandra Camp. She it was who had been responsible for so much of the reorganization of the Corps and all that that entailed. She was Col E. M. B. Dyson, who had been Matron of the Bowen Road Hospital in Hong Kong when the Colony fell to the Japanese. The Parade Commander was Major E. M. Turner, as Dame Margot was in 1950. As from 1 February, 1949, all members of the QARANC became legally eligible for protection by the signatories of the Geneva Convention.

1950 also saw the change from the old ATS ranks to those of the army. Queen Mary agreed to be Colonel-in-Chief of the Corps on 5 April and asked to be told when the King had approved the title. The Nurses' Memorial Chapel in the little Jesus Chapel in Westminster Abbey, unused for three hundred years, was unveiled and dedicated in November. The Queen (now Queen Elizabeth, the Queen Mother) performed the ceremony and the Dean of Westminster dedicated it to the Glory of God. In the rush towards their future, the QAs had not forgotten their own past. A marble plaque commemorating the members of the QAIMNS, the Reserves and TANS had already been unveiled by the CIGS, Field-Marshal Sir William Slim, and dedicated by the Chaplain General in the Chapel at Millbank in 1949.

In 1951 the first QA other ranks were drafted outside the United Kingdom. They went to the BMH in Iserlohn in Germany, and the band of the 1st Battalion, The Queen's Royal Regiment welcomed them. It was that regiment which had had its own hospital in Tangier, one of the first towns the British Army had garrisoned, in the seventeenth century.

In 1952 QA other ranks went east of Suez, to Singapore, to continue their training in the BMH, before becoming State Registered. Later that year some went to Hong Kong.

1952 was the year of the Golden Jubilee of the QAs, but the sad death of King George VI prevented the celebrations taking place on 27 March. However, there was a week of celebrations in June, and on 4 June a Ceremonial Parade took place at the Hindhead Depot and Training Establishment at which four former Matrons-in-Chief were present, Dame Ann Beadsmore Smith, Miss Medforth, Dame Katharine Jones and Dame Louisa Wilkinson. At this parade the QA other ranks wore their new grey uniform for the first time. Hitherto they had worn the same uniforms as the WRAC but with scarlet and grey lanyard and QA shoulder tabs and badges. The Corps wrote, and produced a pageant which was performed on that day.

In October Queen Mary wrote, from Marlborough House, a Foreword to the last book Ian Hay (Major-Gen J. H. Beith) ever wrote, *One Hundred Years of Army Nursing*. It commemorated some of the long series of events in the field of military nursing 'since the leadership of Florence Nightingale', as Queen Mary put it. It was published in 1953.

In March of that year Queen Mary died and again QA Day was postponed. Queen Mary's funeral was on 29 March, two days later. Her Corps kept their own Day on 13 April that year. Nineteen of them marched in the late Queen's funeral procession, together with representatives from The Queen's Royal Regiment and the Queen's Own Rifles of Canada, of which she had also been Colonel-in-Chief, and a contingent of Queen Alexandra's Royal Naval Nursing Service of which she was President.

For over a year the QAs were without a Colonel-in-Chief. During that period they were on parade in London again, taking part in the Coronation procession of Queen Elizabeth II, in June 1953. The Matron-in-Chief, Dame Helen Gillespie was in Westminster Abbey with Dame Louisa Wilkinson. When the QAIMNS became a Corps, following army precedent a Controller Commandant had been appointed and Dame Louisa was chosen. Then, when the rank titles were changed in 1950, the Controller Commandant became Colonel Commandant and it was in that capacity that Dame Louisa was in the Abbey with Dame Helen.

Since Dame Louisa's tenure of office, the post of Colonel Commandant has always been held by a retired Matron-in-Chief but she does not necessarily have to have held the most senior serving position in the Corps. Indeed, it was announced at the end of July, 1974, that Colonel Joan Orford, formerly the army's chief nursing tutor, was to be Dame Margot Turner's successor as Colonel Commandant.

Dame Louisa it was who had formed the QAIMNS Association, again following army precedent, in the year prior to her retirement as Matron-in-Chief. The name was changed to the QARANC Association on 1 February, 1949, and the Association's first Gazette was published in January 1950.

Dame Louisa's name is connected with much of the history of the QAs. She joined the QAIMNS (R) in August 1914. She married in 1917 but her husband was killed shortly afterwards, and in 1919 she became a regular. She served in two world wars from the beginning to the end of each as a serving QA.

A Coronation Year Pageant took place in October in the Royal Festival Hall organized by the Educational Fund Appeal of the Royal College of Nursing. It was called 'They Carry the Torch' and there were two performances. The speaking parts were taken by actors and actresses, but civil nurses took part in the Pageant and there were also representatives of the three Nursing Services present. Florence Nightingale and Scutari were, as might have been expected, dramatically featured.

In June, 1954, as part of the Florence Nightingale Centenary celebrations, a Searchlight Tattoo was held at the White City Stadium in aid of SSAFA, in which the QAs took a prominent part. St Thomas's Hospital lent Miss Nightingale's carriage and a young QA officer,* who had trained at St Thomas's rode in it, impersonating Miss Nightingale and dressed in clothes of the time of the Crimean War.

On 29 September of that year it was announced that the QAs were to have a Colonel-in-Chief again: HRH Princess Margaret. The Corps were delighted.

Queen Alexandra and Queen Mary had each taken a personal

* Now Col Joan Moriarty.

interest and active participation in their activities, and Princess Margaret quickly proved that she was to do the same. On 4 November, less than two months after her appointment, she went to the Thanksgiving Service at Westminster Abbey for the life of Florence Nightingale. Three hundred officers and junior ranks were in the Abbey, with their new Colonel-in-Chief, together with representatives of the sixty-one regiments who had fought in the Crimea. Dame Helen Gillespie laid a wreath at the foot of the Florence Nightingale statue in Waterloo Place and QAs paraded and marched from the Crimean Memorial in Broad Sanctuary to the Abbey.

The Florence Nightingale Centenary Celebrations appropriately extended to Turkey. Two QA officers went to Ankara and Istanbul on 3 and 4 November and formally presented the Governor of Istanbul with a photograph of Florence Nightingale to hang in Scutari Barracks. Correspondence in *The Times* — the paper whose columns could be said to have started it all a hundred years before – in June 1973, revealed that the lamp in the carefully preserved room at Scutari in which Miss Nightingale worked is not the one she actually carried round the wards, although it is of the correct type and period, a Turkish candle lantern. She herself did all she could to dispel the legend of the Lady with the Lamp, but such legends die hard and in the pageants in which QAs have taken part she is invariably depicted carrying one.

But the QAs were by no means solely involved with processions and pageants. Although the Korean War, which had started in 1950, had increased recruiting, the Corps was still below strength and it was not easy always to ensure that the Sisters were where they were needed most, at the bedside. The bedside in the Korean War was an uncomfortable place indeed, and the QAs serving with the Commonwealth Division were on active service again.

Air evacuation of the wounded had been fairly common practice during the Second World War; in Korea it was used exclusively when taking the sick and wounded to Japan. The benefits were great: the Medical Air Evacuation Service, undertaken by the Royal Australian Air Force, relieved the Field Hospitals of congestion and this speedy removal from the battle area did much for morale.

So it was that barely five years after VJ Day the QAs were back in Japan at the BMH in Kure. There were three Matrons – Australian, Canadian and the QARANC. They each had their own staffs. Not for the first time the QAs were working with colleagues from the Commonwealth, and sharing a Mess. Because of different customs, integration had to be worked at; for instance, the Canadians disliked eating the Australian mutton, and many of the conversational expressions used by the Sisters from the two Dominions were as unfamiliar to the QAs as to the other party.

There were no nurses from New Zealand – the unit fighting in Korea was a small one – but the links between the QAs and the New Zealand Army Nursing Service were as strong as they were with the nursing services of the other Dominions. Indeed, in June 1954, while the Canadians, Australians and 'Brits' were working together in Kure, the New Zealanders adopted a uniform which is a copy of the one designed by Norman Hartnell for the QARANC, with the hat designed by Aage Thaarup. An alliance between the QARANC and the NZANS had been approved by George VI in 1949, and in 1966 the Royal New Zealand Nursing Corps adopted QA Day, as RNZNC Day.

It is now common practice for QAs to go to the Dominions on Commonwealth Exchange tours of duty, a liaison which dates back to the South African War when they first nursed the armed forces of the Crown together.

During 1954 five QA NCOs successfully passed the SRN examination. Three of them applied for commissions, for which they were now eligible. Their applications were accepted and they thus became the first members from the other ranks to be commissioned into their own Corps.

QAs were now serving in troopships as well as in the Far East, Germany, the Middle and Near East, Jamaica, Bermuda and West and East Africa. And members of the Reserve were willing to go with the regulars to Suez in 1956. The country was divided about the merits of that expedition, but, as ever, the QAs went where the Army went.

Many members of the Reserve reported, as instructed, to the Depot at Hindhead and the sudden influx caused considerable catering difficulties. It was the first time the permanent staff at Hindhead had had to cope with what appeared at the time to be a national emergency.

Stories are told, and they get better with the telling, of how such was the respect the members of the Reserve had for the 'buff envelopes' containing their orders that some of them arrived with dogs, one with her husband, another with her chickens and another wearing a long grey cloak dating back to the First World War. Apocryphal though these tales may be, they illustrate the eagerness to go wherever the army is sent. In fact, twelve QAs reached Port Said and many more went to Cyprus, where the casualties of the seven day enterprise were taken.

In the same year three senior QA officers went to Rawalpindi and Lahore to be seconded to the Pakistan Armed Forces to assist in the reorganization of their Military Nursing Service. Pakistan had become an Islamic Republic within the Commonwealth in March 1956. At the time of the partition, in 1947, Dame Monica Johnson had been the last QA to leave India. The Ladies of India, in recognition of the nursing services rendered to the Dominion down the years by the QAs gave her a carved chest at the Gateway of India in Bombay which now stands at the head of the stairs, on the first floor, of the Headquarters Mess in Aldershot.

QA officers were seconded, during the late nineteen-fifties and early sixties, to Nigeria, Ghana and Sierra Leone until those countries had established their own Military Nursing Services. Nursing officers from all three countries still continue to come to the QARANC Training Centre to attend courses.

Nearer home, in 1957, QAs were serving in Paris when the Military Hospital was opened in the Hertford British Hospital, providing sixty beds for servicemen with SHAPE and, when there was a SHAPE conference in 1958 a hundred-bedded hospital was flown to France and set up in under two hours. Both

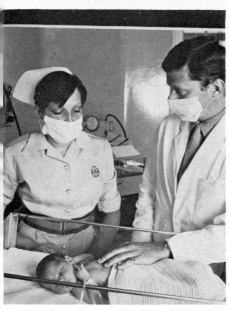

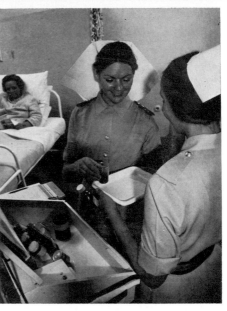

25. *A QARANC sergeant with a captain, RAMC, and a baby in the Infant Care Centre at the Louise Margaret Maternity Hospital, Aldershot, 1973.*

26. *A QARANC captain and corporal working together in the families ward of the British Military Hospital, Rinteln, Germany, in 1973.*

27. *The participants in the QA pageant in honour of 70 years' service held at the Festival of Remembrance, Royal Albert Hall, 1972. The uniforms worn belong to the following periods (left to right): 1939–45, 1939–45, 1972, 1900, Florence Nightingale in 1854, 1902, 1914–18, 1914–18.*

28. *A QARANC corporal and her Gurkha patient on a balcony of the British Military Hospital, overlooking the harbour, Hong Kong, 1973.*

QA officers and trainee nurses were involved in that demonstration.

Trained as the QAs had long been to keep medical records of their patients, they were also mindful of their own historical record, but it was not until the late nineteen-fifties that their possessions, documents, old uniforms and trophies were sufficiently well organized and catalogued for them to have their own museum. It was opened by Princess Margaret at the Depot at Hindhead on 22 May, 1959. On this occasion the Corps presented their Colonel-in-Chief with a gold, diamond, ruby and sapphire brooch in the form of the badge of the Corps. It was a formal military occasion, with a Guard of Honour and music supplied by the RAMC band. It was also a happy occasion for the QAs as they recalled the nursing activities of their past.

Two months earlier the first non-nursing officer had been commissioned into the Corps. After attending the WRAC School of Instruction at Hindhead, WOI Margaret Stephenson became a Lieutenant, QARANC. At the Commissioning Ceremony, following a Drumhead Service, 'Grey and Scarlet' was played. It was a graceful gesture on the part of the WRAC to the first non-nursing officer of their elder sister Corps.

The next year saw the marriage of Princess Margaret to Mr Antony Armstrong-Jones and her Corps gave her presents dating from a period long before QAs had been thought of: a pair of 1829 meat dishes and a pair of 1816 silver sauceboats. The QA Association, of which she was Patron, gave her a Coalport tea service and a set of silver and enamel teaspoons. By this time Dame Helen Gillespie had become Colonel Commandant and Dame Monica Johnson was Matron-in-Chief. They were both at the wedding, as were ten other QAs.

The Corps served in other troubled places after the Second World War besides Korea and Suez. They were in Malaya during the Emergency in the nineteen-fifties and later served in Borneo. They also went to one place where the public might not have expected them to go – Peking. A few had been there in pre-war, and pre-penicillin, days and extra nurses had been sent up from Shanghai in wintertime when the British troops stationed there

H

were particularly subject to pneumonia. Such a situation did not, of course, exist in 1958, the year in which a QA was seconded to the Foreign Office to look after the staff and families of the British Embassy. Her duties were similar to those of a health visitor; she went as a volunteer and, for the period of her appointment – each QA went for a period of two years – she remained there in a civilian capacity. It was not the first time that QAs had looked after non-military personnel in unusual and historic times. The Cultural Revolution took place at a time when one of them was there.

In October 1970, it was announced in the Press by Army Public Relations that QAs were in Jordan. They had gone in September as part of the British section of an International Red Cross relief team, and they wore civilian clothes, bearing the Red Cross badge. No 2 Field Hospital was on stand-by when the call came to be ready to leave. It left the United Kingdom twenty-four hours later. The four QAs flew to Jordan in company with the RAMC and a dental officer. They set up their fifty-bedded hospital in the then unfinished King Hussein Hospital building, about nine miles from the centre of Amman. No 2 Field Hospital got the generators to work and it took one day to clean the building and set up their equipment. They were operational in exactly sixteen hours.

On 1 October the QAs went on duty in the wards at 7.30 in the morning. The first patient, a civilian Jordanian woman, was admitted at eleven o'clock. Forty-eight hours later fifty patients had been admitted.

During the month that followed the RAMC and the QAs looked after sick and wounded members of the Jordanian Army, as well as guerrillas and women and children. The situation in Jordan at that time was such that the period elapsing from the time of wounding until admittance to the hospital varied from approximately forty-eight hours to fourteen days. The majority of patients were therefore suffering from gross infection. When there were insufficient beds to accommodate the patients, the stretcher cases were laid between them. There were language difficulties to be overcome, quite apart from feeding and laundry problems. A tented kitchen was set up in the grounds of the hospital and maintenance flights from Cyprus were provided by the RAF. The QAs' own laundry was taken and returned by the same method.

Not all the patients were wounded; an unharmed Jordanian baby was delivered in the hospital. Her mother, however, had gunshot wounds in the spine and her legs were paralysed. British soldiers made a crib for the baby and gave the mother a bunch of flowers. The baby was named Hope.

No 2 Field Hospital returned to England early in November, having handed over its patients to the Finns, and to Arab nurses.

Before 1970 a less spectacular but highly significant event had taken place in the history of the Corps. The first Gurkha recruits enlisted in Singapore, were brought to England and arrived at Queen Alexandra Camp in November, 1962.

Since the days of Lord Roberts there had always been a particularly close bond between the Gurkhas and the QAs and now, at last, Gurkha girls were part of the Corps. It had taken sixty years. More recruits reached the Depot and Training Establishment at Hindhead the following year, via Singapore. That there are both officers and other ranks from Nepal in and joining the QARANC is now a happily accepted fact.

In 1961 the first pupils started their Part I Midwifery Training at the Louise Margaret Hospital; four were officers and four were sergeants. Both officers and sergeants under such training are now known as 'pupil midwives'. Not many years were to pass before Gurkha QAs who had qualified in the Corps were to go to the Louise Margaret to qualify as midwives themselves.

For some years the need for a new premises for the Depot and Training Centre had been felt. Various sites were visited and, at last, the ideal position was found in a place long associated with the army and with military hospitals, Aldershot. It was also closely associated with the Royal Family, for the site was that of the Royal Pavilion.

It had been built for Queen Victoria. The Prince Consort had chosen the place in 1855, instructing a young subaltern to ride round the site and mark the boundary by dropping pea sticks.

The army had bought eight thousand acres of heathland on the outskirts of Aldershot a few years previously and The Camp, the home and training ground of the army, had come into being.

The Royal Pavilion was built as the place where the Queen would stay when she reviewed her troops. She had a genuine affection for her soldiers: she also had an affection for Aldershot and the Royal Pavilion. George V was the last monarch to stay regularly in the wooden, chalet-type house. He was staying there, with Edward VII, for his father's Coronation Review in 1902 when the King was taken ill and rushed to London by ambulance. Queen Alexandra took the salute in her husband's place at the Review, the year the Army Military Nursing Service took her name.

On the occasion of the last big Review, George V's Silver Jubilee Review in 1935, the King and Queen Mary did not stay at the Royal Pavilion, for the then Duke and Duchess of Gloucester were living there. The King and Queen came down from London and Queen Mary surprised the hundreds of onlookers in the Rushmoor Arena by appearing at the saluting base without her husband. Then the King, in the uniform of a Field-Marshal, rode into the arena, followed by his four sons and the parade of the British Army followed them. Queen Mary, as her mother-in-law had done before her, took the salute.

As well as being in an ideal position it was historically appropriate that the QAs should be based at the Royal Pavilion, Aldershot. The old building was pulled down and on 16 May, 1963, the Colonel-in-Chief, Princess Margaret, Countess of Snowdon arrived in a helicopter of the Queen's Flight, landing on the sports ground near the site to lay the foundation stone.

Dame Barbara Cozens, the Matron-in-Chief, and Dame Monica Golding (neé Johnson), the Colonel Commandant, were both present, and the work of the new building was dedicated by the Assistant Chaplain General.

The stone was an enormous one, approximately fifteen feet in diameter and weighing eight tons. It was lowered into position by a compressed air system which the Princess worked by pulling a lever.

Four years later only the tunnel which had connected the kitchens to the old Royal Pavilion remained and the new Royal Pavilion was standing in the gardens designed by Queen Victoria and the Prince Consort. Around the Foundation Stone, with its inscription and badge of the QARANC in the centre, the new Depot and Training Establishment has been erected from pre-cast concrete panels. It is a purpose-built edifice, designed by the architect Robert Smart, and it has an air of elegance as well as practicality.

Princess Margaret opened the Royal Pavilion on 17 October, 1967. Dame Barbara Cozens had by this time become Colonel Commandant and Dame Margot Turner was Matron-in-Chief. The Colonel-in-Chief unveiled a commemorative bronze plaque on the outer wall of the Officers' Mess. The RAMC Band played 'Grey and Scarlet', the Princess made a tour of inspection and spent some time in the Museum in its new site and in the new Headquarters Mess, as the Royal Pavilion had also become, which was in full working operation.

Here it is that the new recruits come for three weeks preliminary training, where they are given lectures on how to live in a community, on welfare and on administration as it is applied in military hospitals. They are nurses in embryo. There are corporals' and sergents' courses too. State Registered Nurses attend as well, for three weeks, to learn about the army, having received their Commissions on the first day of the course; furthermore there are special courses for junior and more senior officers.

It is from the Royal Pavilion that the new QAs of all ranks go to the Garrison Church in Aldershot for a Service of Dedication before going out into the military hospitals to do the work they joined the Corps to do.

Their forebears, members of the QAIMNS, were a dedicated Service even though they had no Dedication Service; their tradition remains in the Corps today. So does the tradition of the QAIMNS (R) and the TANS, amalgamated now into the TAVR.

The life of the Nursing Board, which had originally been an advisory board, continued beyond the formation of the

QARANC. However, it was gradually realized that it was, through changed circumstances, no longer essential. The Corps had all the nursing and medical contacts it needed in the civil world through its vital relations with the Royal College of Nursing, the General Nursing Council and, indeed, the National Health Service. The Nursing Board had ceased to sit fortnightly for some considerable time when it met for the last time in 1970.

At the Royal Herbert Hospital QAs work in wards from which can be seen the helicopter pad on which the wounded from Northern Ireland arrive. In Nepal they work in the BMH at Dharan which was opened for Gurkhas and their families in 1960; at Netley they tend the sick with colleagues from the other services at the psychiatric hospital. In October 1972, at Colchester Military Hospital, where the first Mess for QA officers to be built in the United Kingdom was opened in 1956, they provided back-up facilities for the Ugandan Asian Resettlement Board; the hospital took in some twenty-nine Ugandan Asians, of whom fourteen were sick. The rest were relatives, and the QAs looked after them all.

The work and dedication of the QA is still not always confined to the nursing of the British army, but wherever the army is, in times of calm and in times of acute trouble, within and without the realm, the QAs are there, and the army and their families are glad of it.

In November 1972, the seventieth year of their existence, the QAs appeared at the Festival of Remembrance at the Royal Albert Hall, dressed in uniforms of various periods supplied by the QARANC Museum, including, inevitably, that of Scutari. The packed building echoed with cheers as they came into the arena. Brig Barbara Gordon, the first woman to become a Companion of the Order of the Bath (Military Division), was Matron-in-Chief at the time, and she played no small part in ensuring that the Corps participated in the Festival of Remembrance in their seventieth birthday year.

The following year Brig Helen Cattanach, a holder of the Royal Red Cross, as had been all her predecessors from the days of Dame Sydney Browne, succeeded her as Matron-in-Chief and

Director of Army Nursing Services. In the same year the QARANC, together with the RAMC and the RADC, were given the Freedom of Aldershot. The ceremony took place on 27 June, 1973. The Scroll conveying the Freedom, and a silver casket in which to keep it, was presented to the Casket Bearer and trooped through the Parade in slow time, accompanied by the Casket Guard. The Freedom was received on behalf of the Army Medical Services by the DGAMS, Lt-Gen Sir James Baird. The parade consisted of five companies, the fourth of which was supplied by QAs from the QARANC Training Centre, the Louise Margaret Maternity Hospital and the Cambridge Military Hospital. It was commanded by Major Margaret Stephenson, who had been the first non-nursing officer to be commissioned into the Corps.

The Mayor, in his address, spoke of these two military hospitals in Aldershot, and the many who had received help and kindness from them. He said, too, that he was the last Mayor of Aldershot, for under the new Council (to come into being in 1974) the area would be known as Rushmoor, the name of the Arena where so many parades of former years had taken place. As the companies left the parade ground to march through the streets of Aldershot, 'Grey and Scarlet' was the last tune to be played in the March Past.

A signal honour had been conferred upon the Army Medical Services by the town known as the Home of the British Army. One QA officer who was there said that 27 June, 1973, was a 'dull but warm day – ideal for parades and standing around'. She knew that, efficiently though they may have learned to take part in them, parades are not the main functions of the QARANC. QAs are nurses first and soldiers second – and women most of all. As for standing around, she knew very well that no QA has ever joined the Corps to do that.

And we who know them know that too.

APPENDIX A

QAIMNS Matrons-in-Chief

Dame Sidney Jane Browne, GBE, RRC. 1902–1906
Miss Caroline Helen Keer, RRC and Bar. 1906–1910
Dame Ethel Hope Becher, GBE, RRC and Bar. 1910–1919
Dame Ann Beadsmore Smith, DBE, RRC and Bar. 1919–1924
Miss Florence May Hodgins, CBE, RRC and Bar. 1924–1928
Miss Rosabelle Osborne, CBE, RRC. 1928–1930
Miss Marguerite Elizabeth Medforth, CBE, RRC. 1930–1934
Miss Daisy Maud Martin, CBE, RRC. 1934–1938
Miss Catherine Murray Roy, CBE, RRC, MM. 1938–1940
Dame Katharine Henrietta Jones, DBE, RRC and Bar. 1940–1944
Dame Louisa Jane Wilkinson, DBE, RRC. 1944–1948
Miss Anne Thomson, CBE, RRC. 1948–31 January, 1949

QARANC Matrons-in-Chief (Army) and Directors of Army Nursing Services

Brig Dame Anne Thomson, DBE, RRC, KHNS. 1 February, 1949–1952
Brig Dame Helen Shiels Gillespie, DBE, RRC, QHNS. 1952–1956
Brig Dame Monica Johnson, DBE, RRC, QHNS. 1956–1960
Brig Dame Barbara Cozens, DBE, RRC, QHNS. 1960–1964
Brig Dame Margot Turner, DBE, RRC, QHNS. 1964–1968
Brig Barbara Masson Gordon, CB, RRC, QHNS. 1968–1973
Brig Helen Cattanach, RRC, QHNS. 1973–

APPENDIX B

The Corps March

'GREY AND SCARLET'

In June, 1948, Lt-Gen Sir Neil Cantlie suggested that the QAs should have a special tune for their March Past, and by 1950 'Grey and Scarlet' had been adopted as the Corps March. It was first played in public on 13 September, 1950, at the opening of the new QARANC Depot and Training Establishment at Hindhead. 'Grey and Scarlet' was arranged by Capt L. D. Brown, then Director of Music, RAMC, and consists of Purcell's 'King Arthur' followed by the traditional air, 'Gentle Maiden'.